ANNEX

The Music Hour

in the

Kindergarten and First Grade

by

Osbourne McConathy

Formerly Director of the Department of Public School Music, Northwestern University

W. Otto Miessner

Chairman, Department of School Music, School of Fine Arts
University of Kansas

Edward Bailey Birge

Professor of Public School Music, Indiana University

Mabel E. Bray

Director of Music, New Jersey State Teachers College
Trenton, New Jersey

Silver Burdett Company

New York   Boston   Chicago   San Francisco

The Music Hour

Grade-by-grade Series

KINDERGARTEN AND FIRST GRADE, a book for the teacher, containing songs, activities, and directions, 224 pages

FIRST BOOK, 112 pages

SECOND BOOK, 144 pages

THIRD BOOK, 160 pages

FOURTH BOOK, 176 pages

FIFTH BOOK, 192 pages

ELEMENTARY TEACHER'S BOOK to accompany the First and Second Books, 280 pages, with accompaniments and additional rote songs

INTERMEDIATE TEACHER'S BOOK to accompany the Third and Fourth Books, 416 pages, with accompaniments

TEACHER'S GUIDE FOR THE FIFTH BOOK, 352 pages, with accompaniments

For one- and two-room schools and ungraded schools

ONE–BOOK COURSE, 232 pages

ACCOMPANIMENTS FOR SONGS in the One-Book Course, 144 pages

TWO–BOOK COURSE
  LOWER GRADES, 152 pages
  UPPER GRADES, 200 pages

ACCOMPANIMENTS FOR SONGS in the Two-Book Course, 208 pages

MUSIC IN RURAL EDUCATION, teacher's book for the One-Book Course and the Two-Book Course, 320 pages

WHAT THE TEACHER SHOULD KNOW, introductory pamphlet for the One-Book Course and the Two-Book Course, 48 pages

Junior High School or upper grammar grades

MUSIC HIGHWAYS AND BYWAYS (" The Bronze Book "), 256 pages

MUSIC OF MANY LANDS AND PEOPLES (" The Silver Book "), 272 pages

507514

TO THE TEACHERS
WHO BRING MUSIC INTO THE LIVES
OF LITTLE CHILDREN

FOREWORD

The spirit of play and the imaginative world of little children are delightfully and vividly expressed through music. Music is a stimulating force which appeals to children; it vitalizes their daily lives; it arouses and satisfies their desire for rhythmic expression; it creates and develops moods; it intensifies moods already created; and it is one of the most potent means for promoting social relationships.

The wealth of songs, rhythms and selections for music appreciation in THE MUSIC HOUR IN THE KINDERGARTEN AND FIRST GRADE, together with the toy orchestra activities, supplies the inspiration for a rich experience which will serve as a foundation for future musical growth.

The appeal of rhythms in music is recognized to be of special importance in these years, and the songs, as well as the instrumental music, are in simple, swinging rhythms suitable to children of this age. The melodies are all simple, and though brief and tuneful, preserve artistic balance and proportion. The material of this book covers such a wide variety of subjects that all phases of early child life are illustrated as they occur in the year's school program.

Because of the closer relationship which is being sought between the kindergarten and the first grade (and extending to the other primary grades) it is not only desirable but essential that the teachers of each of the two lowest classes know the material and procedure of the other class. In fact, much of the material is and should be interchangeable, the *topic* being the chief determining factor in the choice of songs and of music to be heard. For the convenience of the teachers of the two beginning classes, the material for both has been incorporated in this one book.

The spirit of the kindergarten, with its freedom and its close relation to child life should be retained in the music of the first grade, and wherever possible the piano and phonograph should be used in connection with the daily topics of the class and in connection with the rhythmic activities of the children. This is the first book in which a definitely correlated program of music has been provided for the kindergarten and first grade. It is intended to meet the needs of children as they first come to school and to give them that background which will prepare them for the music program of succeeding years.

Osbourne McConathy

W. Otto Miessner

Edward B. Birge

Mabel E. Bray

ACKNOWLEDGMENTS

The courtesy of the following authors and publishers in allowing the use of copyrighted material is gratefully acknowledged:

Messrs. Bayley and Ferguson for the "Old French Minuet" from *Characteristic Songs and Dances of All Nations* arranged by Alfred Moffat.

The Bobbs-Merrill Company for "Extremes" by James Whitcomb Riley from *The Book of Joyous Children*, copyright, 1902, and "A Sea Song from the Shore" by James Whitcomb Riley from *Poems Here at Home*, copyright, 1893–1920. Used by special permission of the publishers.

Samuel E. Cassino for "Kris Kringle's Travels" by Susie M. Best.

The Century Company for "Ironing Song" by Bessie Hill and "Concerning Travel" by Caroline Hofman from the *St. Nicholas Magazine*, and "My Baby-Bo" by Laura E. Richards from *St. Nicholas Songs*.

Thomas Charles Company for the poems "Taddy Pole and Polly Wog" and "Five Little White Mice" from *Songs, Games and Rhymes* published by The Milton Bradley Company.

Child Life Magazine for "Clouds" by Helen de Lorenzi; "Rain in April" by Eleanor Hammond; "March" by Louise Ayres Garnett; and "The Willow Cats" by Margaret Widdemer; by special permission of the authors and the publishers, Rand McNally and Company.

Doubleday, Doran and Company for "The Fountain" from *Fairies and Chimneys* by Rose Fyleman, copyright, 1926, by George H. Doran Company.

Educational Publishing Corporation for "The Field Daisy" from *Complete Holiday Program* by H. M. Burns and M. C. Nunnery.

Houghton Mifflin Company for "Jack-in-the-Pulpit" by Clara Smith from *Child-Life in Poetry* by John Greenleaf Whittier and Lucy Larcom.

Little, Brown and Company for "The Pet Rabbit" by Robert E. Mack from *The Child's Harvest of Verse*.

Longmans, Green and Company for "My Dog" by E. Gordon Browne from *A Bunch of Blossoms*.

Lothrop, Lee and Shepard Company for "Who Likes the Rain" by Clara Doty Bates from *The Child's Harvest of Verse* published by Little, Brown and Company.

The Macmillan Company for "The Dragon," "The Little Goblin," and "I Wish" from *The Golden Trumpets* by Blanche Jennings Thompson.

F. A. Owen Publishing Company for "My Kite" by Maude M. Grant and "A Christmas Song" by Virginia Baker from *Choice Pieces for Primary Pupils*.

Henry R. Pattengill, publisher, and the author, for "Morning" from *Farmerkin's Farm Rhymes* by Dora H. Stockman.

The Penn Publishing Company for "I am the Wind" from *New Year and Midwinter Exercises* by Alice M. Kellogg by permission of and arrangement with the publishers.

James B. Pinker and Sons for "Ann's Teeth" by Walter de la Mare from *A Child's Day*, and "The Cupboard" and "Bread and Cherries" by Walter de la Mare from *Peacock Pie* published by Henry Holt and Company.

The Public School Publishing Company for "November" from *Songs of the Tree Top and Meadow*.

G. P. Putnam's Sons for "The Robin" by Laurence Alma-Tadema from Chisholm's *The Golden Staircase*, and "Sing, Said the Mother" from *English Folk Songs from the Southern Appalachians* collected by Olive Dame Campbell and Cecil J. Sharp.

Fleming H. Revell Company for "Old Mother Wind" and "The Old Woman" by Isaac Taylor Headland from *Chinese Mother Goose Rhymes*.

Schroeder and Gunther, Inc., for the "Little Waltz" by R. S. Ambrose from "Synthetic Series, No. 88."

Charles Scribner's Sons for "At the Seaside," "The Land of Counterpane," and "The Friendly Cow" from *A Child's Garden of Verses* by Robert Louis Stevenson, and "Snowflakes" by Mary Mapes Dodge.

The Viking Press for "The Rabbit" by Elizabeth Madox Roberts from *Under the Trees*, copyright, 1922, B. W. Huebsch, Inc.

Grateful acknowledgment is due the Metropolitan Museum of Art for permission to use the picture "Calmady Children" by Sir Thomas Lawrence; and the Art Extension Press, Westport, Connecticut, for permission to reproduce the picture "Calmady Children," and the picture "Don Baltazar Carlos on Horseback" by Velasquez.

Grateful acknowledgment is also due Mrs. Emma Grant Meader of the State Normal School, New Haven, Connecticut, and Teachers College, Columbia University, for her selection and supervision of the choice of poetry; Mrs. Florence E. Dangerfield, Director of the Department of Physical Education, Bradford Academy, Haverhill, Massachusetts, for her assistance in correlating rhythmic activities with the vocal music lesson; Mrs. Shirley Kite Smith for the cover design; and especially the poets and composers who have graciously contributed to the book as an expression of their love for little children.

The Calmady Children, Lawrence (1769-1830)

The Music Hour
in the
Kindergarten and First Grade

PART ONE
The Kindergarten

Autumn Leaves

Nancy Byrd Turner

Anice Terhune

Gaily

The au - tumn leaves are gold and red, They dance like fair - ies o - ver - head, They dance like fair - ies when we sing, They dance all in a fair - y ring, A fair - - - y ring.

I. HOME

Rock-a-Bye

MABEL E. BRAY

OSBOURNE McCONATHY

In swinging rhythm

Rock-a-bye, ba-by, Moth-er is near, Sing-ing and rock-ing Her ba-by dear.

A Baby's Way

MINNIE E. HICKS

ANICE TERHUNE

Tenderly, but not too slowly

I have a ba-by sis-ter, A dar-ling ti-ny mite, And
She's say-ing that she loves me, In that sweet ba-by way, And

when I smile, she smiles at me And holds my fin-ger tight.
ask-ing me to wait a bit 'Till she can run and play.

Morning

DORA H. STOCKMAN

W. OTTO MIESSNER

Brightly

I like to have it morn-ing For as soon as it is day, I

climb so quick-ly out of bed, And hur-ry out to play!

Trot, Trot

MARY F. BUTTS

W. OTTO MIESSNER

Quickly

Ev - 'ry ev - 'ning ba - by goes trot, trot to town;____ A -

cross the riv - er and through the field, Up hill and down.____

Now Good-Night

MABEL E. BRAY

TAPS

Slowly

Now good - night, child - ren dear! Soft - ly sleep, sweet - ly dream, Moth - er's

here. Till the day comes a - gain She is near.

Playing with Baby

NURSERY RHYME

GEORGE L. WRIGHT

Moderato

1. Pat - a - cake, Ba - by, Pat - a - cake; Pat - a - cake, Ba - by, Pat - a - cake!
2. Nod your head, Ba - by, Nod your head, Nod your head, Ba - by, Nod your head.
3. Smile at us, Ba - by, Smile at us, Smile at us,__ Ba - by, Smile at us.

The Sandman

SARAH GRAMES CLARK

EDWARD B. BIRGE

Moderato

There's a wee lit-tle man with a bag of sand Who vis-its you and me, And be-fore he has said a sin-gle word, We're sleep-y as can be.

The Spinner

LOUISE AYRES GARNETT

PAUL AMBROSE

Allegretto

Kit-ty, un-der-neath her fur, Spins her do-zy, co-zy purr,

Like a mo-tor hear it whirr; Purr, purr, purr!

Bow-wow-wow!

MOTHER GOOSE

TRADITIONAL

Moderato

Bow-wow-wow! Whose dog art thou? Lit-tle Tom-my Tink-er's dog. Bow-wow-wow!

Bunny

BLANCHE JENNINGS THOMPSON

DANIEL PROTHEROE

Bun-ny, bun-ny, fun-ny bun-ny, Sit-ting in the gar-den sun-ny.

Here's some cab-bage, let-tuce too,— 'Tis the ver-y best for you.

Bun-ny's an-swer is po-lite,— "Such a treat is a de-light;

Won't you stop,— Won't you stop,— Won't you stop and have a bite?"—

Dish-Washing Song

NANCY BYRD TURNER

GERMAN FOLK SONG

Have the wa-ter— hot and clean, Put the dish-es gen-tly in;

Dry them well and make them shine, Set them on the shelf in line!

Wise Little Gold Fish

GEORGE S. APPLEGARTH

W. OTTO MIESSNER

Moderato

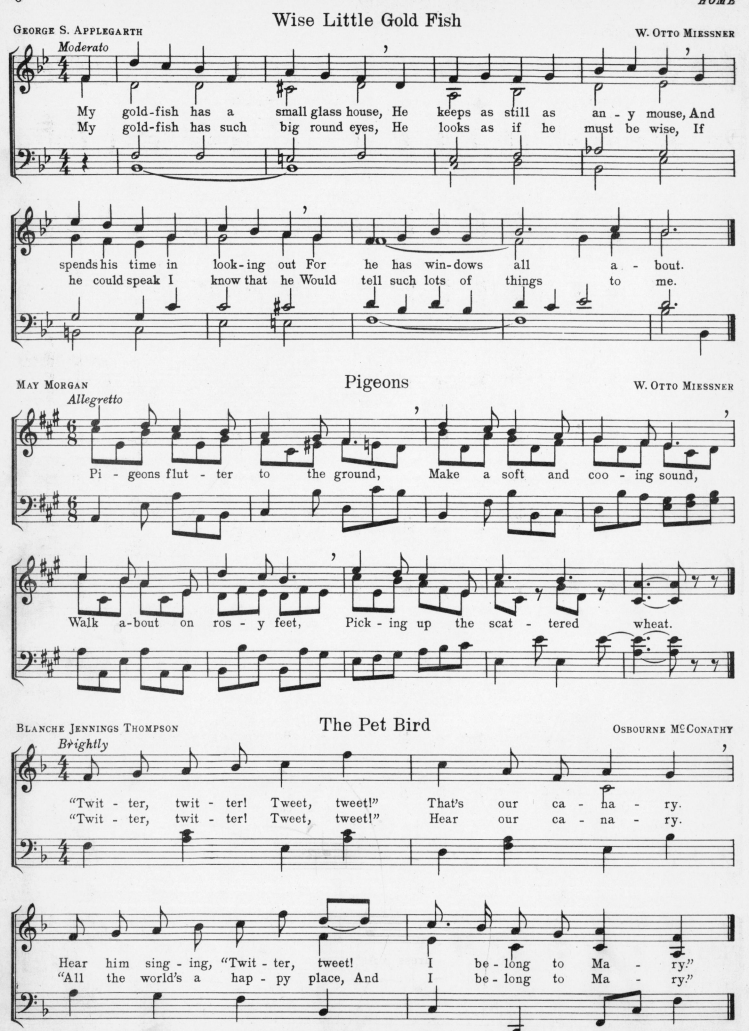

My gold-fish has a small glass house, He keeps as still as an - y mouse, And
My gold-fish has such big round eyes, He looks as if he must be wise, If

spends his time in look-ing out For he has win-dows all a - bout.
he could speak I know that he Would tell such lots of things to me.

Pigeons

MAY MORGAN

W. OTTO MIESSNER

Allegretto

Pi - geons flut - ter to the ground, Make a soft and coo - ing sound,

Walk a-bout on ros - y feet, Pick - ing up the scat - tered wheat.

The Pet Bird

BLANCHE JENNINGS THOMPSON

OSBOURNE McCONATHY

Brightly

"Twit - ter, twit - ter! Tweet, tweet!" That's our ca - na - ry.
"Twit - ter, twit - ter! Tweet, tweet!" Hear our ca - na - ry.

Hear him sing - ing, "Twit - ter, tweet! I be - long to Ma - ry."
"All the world's a hap - py place, And I be - long to Ma - ry."

Washing Day

Agnes Choate Wonson

Edward B. Birge

Allegretto

Mon - day morn I wash the clothes And hang them nice and high;

Dol - ly has to go to bed Un - til they all get dry.

Ironing Day

Bessie Hill

Edward B. Birge

Moderato

First your i - ron smooth must be, Rub a - way,_____ rub a - way!_____
Though your i - ron must be hot, Glide a - way,_____ slide a - way!_____

Rust and i - ron dis - a - gree, Rub a - way,_____ rub a - way!_____
It must nev - er scorch or spot, Glide a - way,_____ slide a - way!_____

Real Work

Aldis Dunbar

G. A. Grant-Schaefer

Moderato

I can sew a seam,_____ I can stitch a hold - er,

I shall make a dol - ly's dress As soon as I am old - er.

The Broom

ELLA D. WATKINS

OSBOURNE McCONATHY

With firm rhythm

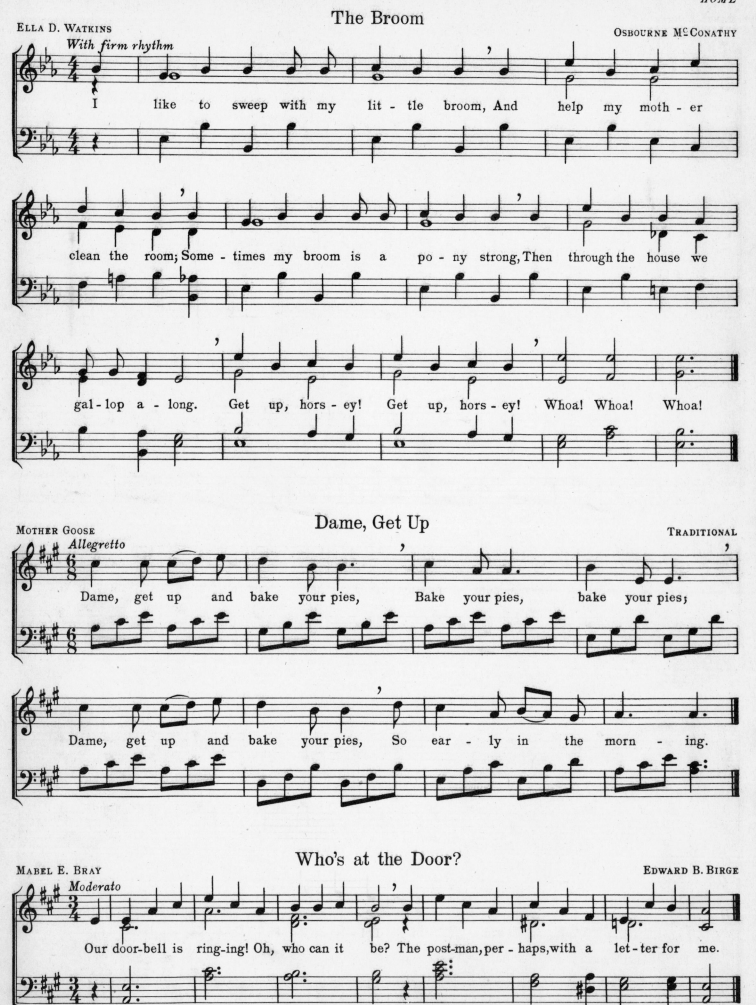

I like to sweep with my lit-tle broom, And help my moth-er clean the room; Some-times my broom is a po-ny strong, Then through the house we gal-lop a-long. Get up, hors-ey! Get up, hors-ey! Whoa! Whoa! Whoa!

Dame, Get Up

MOTHER GOOSE

TRADITIONAL

Allegretto

Dame, get up and bake your pies, Bake your pies, bake your pies; Dame, get up and bake your pies, So ear-ly in the morn-ing.

Who's at the Door?

MABEL E. BRAY

EDWARD B. BIRGE

Moderato

Our door-bell is ring-ing! Oh, who can it be? The post-man, per-haps, with a let-ter for me.

At Tea

MABEL E. BRAY
PAUL AMBROSE

Allegretto

"Good aft - er - noon, good aft - er - noon, I'm glad you came for tea." "Thank you ver - y much in - deed, I'm glad that you asked me."

Animal Crackers

LINN MOORE MILLER
EDWARD B. BIRGE

Briskly

I have the cut - est lit - tle zoo, All bears and li - ons and ti - gers too, And of - ten when there's com - pa - ny, I have an el - e - phant for tea.

The Cupboard

WALTER DE LA MARE
W. OTTO MIESSNER

Moderato

I know a lit - tle cup - board, With a teen - y ti - ny key, And there's a jar of Lol - ly - pops For me, me, me.

Cradle Song

TRADITIONAL

TRADITIONAL

Rock-a-bye, baby, on the tree top, When the wind blows the cra-dle will rock;

When the bough breaks the cra-dle will fall,— Down will come ba - by, cra-dle and all.

Clocks

MABEL E. BRAY

MABEL E. BRAY

(Tick- tock, tick -tock, tick-tock, tick) A clock in the kitch-en, A clock in the hall;

(Piano or teacher- - - - - -)

Some clocks are lit - tle, And some clocks are tall.— (Tick - tick - tick - tick - tock.)

(Piano or teacher- - - - -)

Time to Get Up

NANCY BYRD TURNER

ARMY BUGLE CALL

"Good morn - ing! Good morn - ing!" I hear a rob - in call; "The

sun's up, the sun's up, Come greet him, one and all!"

Before School

ANNA M. SHEPARD

FRENCH FOLK SONG

1. I washed my face like this,___ I washed my face like this,— Ear-ly to-
2. I brushed my teeth like this,___ I brushed my teeth like this,— Ear-ly to-
3. I combed my hair like this,___ I combed my hair like this,— Ear-ly to-
4. I drank my milk like this,___ I drank my milk like this,— Ear-ly to-

day, ear-ly to-day,— Be-fore I came to school, I washed my face like this.___
day, ear-ly to-day,— Be-fore I came to school, I brushed my teeth like this.___
day, ear-ly to-day,— Be-fore I came to school, I combed my hair like this.___
day, ear-ly to-day,— Be-fore I came to school, I drank my milk like this.___

Safety First

LINN MOORE MILLER

LINN MOORE MILLER

Look out! Look out! Be-fore you cross the street; Look up! Look

down! To see what you will meet; And if there are no cars in sight, Then

skip and skip with all your might; Skip, skip, skip, Then skip with all your might.

Ready for School

MABEL E. BRAY

EDWARD A. MUELLER

My blouse is fresh, my shoes are shined; My hair is combed just so; My face and hands are ver-y clean; I'm read-y now to go.

Good Morning, Happy Children

OLD ENGLISH MELODY

Good morn - ing, hap - py chil - dren! An - oth - er day is here,____ For work and rest and play - ing With all our friends so dear.____

Call to Work or Play

MABEL E. BRAY

OLD FRENCH HUNTING CALL

1. Come chil - dren, to your plac - es, It's time to sing a song.____
2. Come chil - dren, to your plac - es, It's time to eat your lunch.____
3. Come chil - dren, to your plac - es, We're going to build a house.____
4. Come chil - dren, to your plac - es, The band is going to play.____

Note: This may be used for any activity.

Good Morning!

ELLA D. WATKINS.   ANICE TERHUNE

Good morn-ing, all, on this new day, In which to sing and work and play; Good

morn-ing, all, good morn-ing all! Good morn-ing all, good morn-ing all!

The Right Way

ANNA M. PRATT   EDWARD B. BIRGE

Work when you work, Play when you play, Cheer-i-ly, mer-ri-ly, that is the way.

Things I Like

W. OTTO MIESSNER   W. OTTO MIESSNER

I like to dance, I like to play, I like to go to school ev-'ry day;

I like to read, I like to sing, I like most ev-'ry-thing.

Going to School in the Rain

ELLA D. WATKINS

L. LESLIE LOTH

Morning Prayer

NANCY BYRD TURNER

THE MODERN MUSIC SERIES

Politeness

VERNETTA F. DECKER

PAUL AMBROSE

Greeting to Visitors

ANNA M. SHEPARD

GEOFFREY O'HARA

How do you do, Miss John - son,* How do you do to - day?___ We're

glad you've come to see us And hope that you can stay.

* Sing name of visitor.

A Good-by Song

NINA B. HARTFORD

NINA B. HARTFORD

Our work is done, it's time to say, "Good-by"___ un - til an - oth - er day.
As home we run with trip - ping feet, We'll look___ be - fore we cross the street.

Children, Good-by

W. OTTO MIESSNER

W. OTTO MIESSNER

Chil - dren, good - by,___ Teach - er, good - by,___ Take all my love with you,

Teach - er, we love you too! Chil - dren, good - by!___ Teach - er, good - by!___

Riding

Agnes Choate Wonson

W. Otto Miessner

Ride a-way East,—— Ride a-way West,—— Ride to the one that you love best.——

Follow the Leader

Mabel E. Bray

Scandinavian Folk Song

Moderato

1. Fol-low me wher-ev-er I go, And do ev-'ry-thing that I tell you to do.——
2. First we walk and then we—— skip, And then we will jump with a clip, clip,—— clip.——
3. Now we'll run a mer-ry—— race, And then we will stop, ev-'ry one in his place.——

Playing in the Band

Frank L. Laird

W. Otto Miessner

In march time

Ta ra ta ta ta, Ta ra ta ta ta, See our band as it comes up the

street!—— Our horns are loud-ly bray-ing, Gay mu-sic we are

play-ing, Ta ra ta, ta ra ta, ta ra ta,—— See our band march-ing up the street!

To Market

MOTHER GOOSE
Moderato

FRENCH NURSERY SONG

To mar-ket, to mar-ket to buy a fat pig; Then home a-gain, home a-gain jig-ge-ty jig.

Playing Circus

VERNETTA F. DECKER
Allegretto

EDWARD B. BIRGE

Fa - ther puts his pa-per down And plays at bear and cir - cus clown. I

wish he'd stay at home all day! He makes good nois - es when we play.

Jack-in-the-Box

MABEL E. BRAY
Quickly

RUSSIAN FOLK SONG

Such a fun - ny thing to play with! See, it un - locks.

Take a - way your fin - ger, Out jumps Jack - in - the - Box!

Little Waltz
(The Bouncing Ball)

R. S. AMBROSE

Note: Music for **bouncing** and **catching** the ball.

Playing Ball

BLANCHE JENNINGS THOMPSON

PAUL AMBROSE

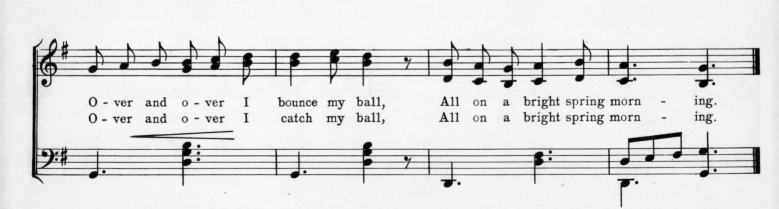

O - ver and o - ver I bounce my ball, Bounce my ball, bounce my ball.
O - ver and o - ver I catch my ball, Catch my ball, catch my ball.

O - ver and o - ver I bounce my ball, All on a bright spring morn - ing.
O - ver and o - ver I catch my ball, All on a bright spring morn - ing.

Waltz from "Love's Dream after the Ball"
(See - Saw)

ALPHONS CZIBULKA

*Note: The first sixteen measures may be repeated.

A Game

OLD NURSERY RHYME

GERMAN FOLK TUNE

Let the feet go tap, tap, tap! Let the hands go clap, clap, clap!

Let the head nod to and fro! Now a - round the room we go!

March
From "Aida"

GIUSEPPE VERDI

D. S. al Fine

The Parade

NINA B. HARTFORD

NINA B. HARTFORD

In marching tempo

Oh, hark! the sol-diers are march-ing, I hear the bu-gle and drum;___ Oh, see! they're turn-ing the cor-ner! We'll cheer them as they come.___

Marching

MABEL E. BRAY

MABEL E. BRAY

In marching tempo

March, march, march, march! Sol-diers in a row!___

Toot, toot, toot, toot! Hear the bu-gles blow!

Street Boys' Parade
(For Marching)

GEORGES BIZET
From "Carmen"

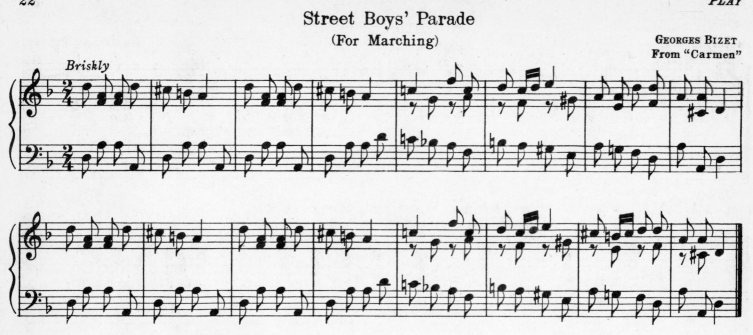

The Knight of the Hobby-horse
(For playing Rocking Horse)

ROBERT SCHUMANN
From "Scenes from Childhood" Op. 15

Two Little Blackbirds

MOTHER GOOSE

OLD GERMAN MELODY

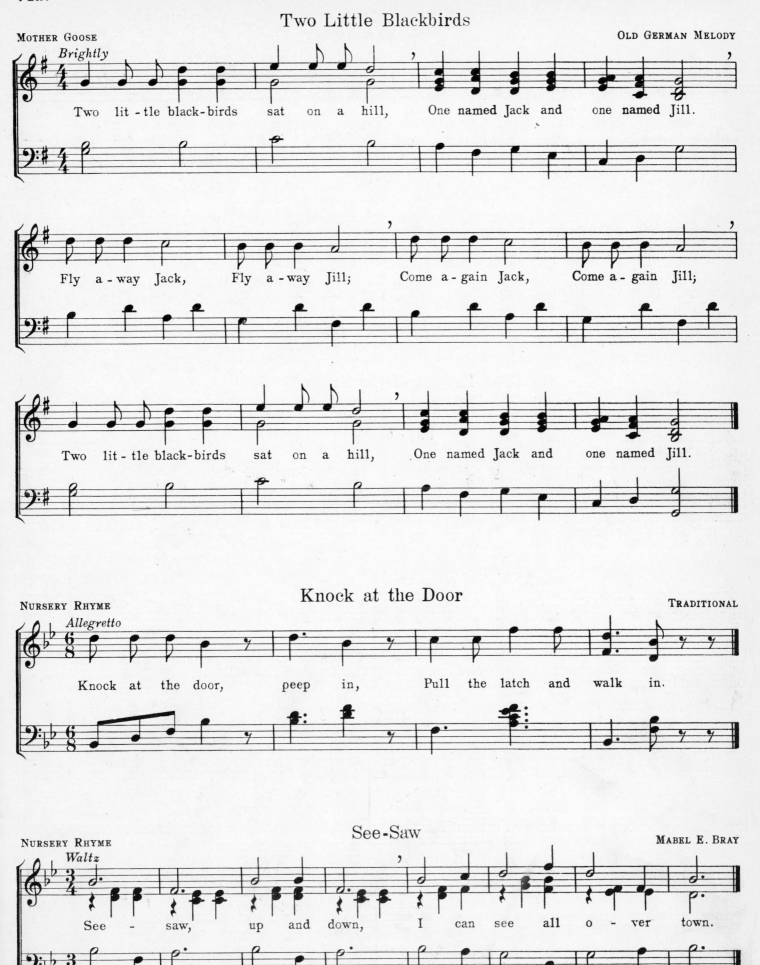

Two lit-tle black-birds sat on a hill, One named Jack and one named Jill.

Fly a-way Jack, Fly a-way Jill; Come a-gain Jack, Come a-gain Jill;

Two lit-tle black-birds sat on a hill, One named Jack and one named Jill.

Knock at the Door

NURSERY RHYME

TRADITIONAL

Knock at the door, peep in, Pull the latch and walk in.

See-Saw

NURSERY RHYME

MABEL E. BRAY

See - saw, up and down, I can see all o - ver town.

The Rocking Horse

FLORENCE C. FOX

EDWARD B. BIRGE

Ride, ride, my hob-ble de ho! Back and forth the rock-ers go! A
hun-dred miles for a po-ny ride, And nev-er a step from Moth-er's side.

Paper Dolls

AGNES CHOATE WONSON

MABEL E. BRAY

One doll, two dolls, Lots in a row; I can cut out man-y more; See my scis-sors go!

Dolly's Lullaby

NINA B. HARTFORD

NINA B. HARTFORD

Dol-ly dar-ling, close your eyes, Tir-ed now and wea-ry;
I will sing a lul-la-by, Go to sleep, my dear-ie.

Sleeping Dolls

JULIA COLTON WILLARD

PAUL AMBROSE

Dol-ly in my arms you're sleep-ing, Lull-a-by, O lull-a-by!

While you sleep a watch I'm keep-ing, Lull-a-by, O lull-a-by!

Lull-a-by, lull-a-lull-a-by;

While you sleep a watch I'm keep-ing, lull-a-lull-a-by.

Whirl, Top, Whirl!

BLANCHE JENNINGS THOMPSON

G. A. GRANT-SCHAEFER

Whirl, top, whirl! And spin, top, spin! That's what you were made for, Spin, top, spin!

My Flute

W. OTTO MIESSNER

W. OTTO MIESSNER

Too-tle, too-tle, toot; Hear me play my flute! I like to play each lit-tle tune, Be-

cause it sounds like birds in June. Too-tle, too-tle, too-tle too-tle, Too-tle too-tle, toot!

My Teddy Bear

AGNES CHOATE WONSON

G. A. GRANT-SCHAEFER

Andante

I have my toys, my train of cars, My au-to and my kit-ty

cat; But Ted-dy Bear is best of all He is so dear and round and fat!

My Fire Engine

AGNES CHOATE WONSON

DANIEL PROTHEROE

Allegretto con spirito

Ring the bell and blow the horn! Boys, look sharp, get out the way! My

big fire en-gine's com-ing; There are lots of fires to-day!

Playing the Bugle

FRENCH HUNTING CALL

Ta, ta, ta, ta, ta, ta, Ta, ta, ta, ta, ta, ta, ta, ta! Ta, ta, ta, ta, ta, ta, Ta, ta, ta, ta, ta, ta, ta, ta.

Church Bells

MABEL E. BRAY

SWEDISH FOLK SONG

Moderato

Teacher and best singers

Bells ring-ing in the church stee-ple high, *Children (or monotones)* Ding, ding, dong! *Teacher* Call to the peo-ple

Children (or monotones) pass - ing by, Ding, ding, dong! *All* "Come to the church," *Monotones* Ding, ding, dong!

All "Come to the church!" *Monotones* Ding, ding, dong! *Teacher and best singers* Hear the sweet bells ring-ing in the stee-ple high!

The Drum

NANCY BYRD TURNER

GERMAN TUNE

In marching tempo

Bum, bum, hear the drum, Bum, bum, hear the drum, Bum, bum, down the street See the

men as they come; Dr - r - r - um, bum, bum, Dr - r - r - um, bum, bum, Dr - r - r - um, bum, bum, Hear the drum!

V. IMITATING ANIMALS
Happy Journey

FRANZ BEHR

Note: Rhythmic activity, high-stepping horses; run and skip.

Arabesque
(Elephants)

G. KARGANOFF

The Elephant

AGNES CHOATE WONSON

G. A. GRANT-SCHAEFER

Mis - ter Wrin - kled El - e - phant, — Are you ver - y old?
Still it's ver - y han - dy To eat with, I sup - pose;

If my nose was long as yours, — I'm a - fraid I'd scold! _____
Here are pea - nuts fresh for you To pick up with your nose! _____

Wee Ducky Doddles

GEORGE S. APPLEGARTH

PAUL AMBROSE

Allegretto

When wee Duck-y Dod-dles Is out on the ground, He wad-dles and tod-dles And stum-bles a-round, But

when he goes swim-ming, O then you should see! No boat can go skim-ming So gai-ly as he.

Note: Repeat piano part for waddling duck action.

The Bear

AGNES CHOATE WONSON

FRANCIS FINDLAY

Moderato

Big bear so growl-y-prowl-y, I know I'm glad to see____ That

you are safe be-hind your bars, And not out here with me!____

poco riten. *a tempo*

Theme from the "First Mazurka"
(The Bear)

CAMILLE SAINT-SAËNS

Vivace

Puss

Louise Ayres Garnett

G. A. Grant-Schaefer

Con moto

Kit-ty-cat, pit-ty-pat, So warm and fur-ry, I'll catch you, pret-ty cat, If you don't hur-ry!

Tin Soldiers and Pussy

Nina B. Hartford

Nina B. Hartford

In marching tempo

Tramp, tramp, tramp, tramp, O-ver the kitch-en floor.___ My
Creep, creep, creep, creep, Pus-sy is back a-gain.___ She

sol-diers fright-ened the pus-sy cat Till she ran out the door.___
pounc-es down on the cap-tain And scat-ters all the men.___

Les Pifferari
(The Rabbit)

Charles Gounod

Quickly

The Squirrel

Author unknown

Paul Ambrose

Frisk - y, brisk - y, hip - pi - ty hop, Up he goes to the tall tree top;

Whirl - y, twirl - y, round and round, Down he scam - pers to the ground.

Allegro in B♭
(Sparrows Hopping)

Wolfgang Amadeus Mozart
(Composed at the age of six)

At the Zoo

SARAH GRAMES CLARK

DANIEL PROTHEROE

Have you ev-er been to vis-it the zoo? A hap-py place for__ me and you; And what did you see? And what did you do? Did the li-on roar when you went to the zoo?

The Merry-Go-Round

VIRGINIA BAKER

SWEDISH SINGING GAME

Oh, cam-els and bears And po-nies are found; All pranc-ing a-bout in the mer-ry-go-round.

My Pony

BLANCHE JENNINGS THOMPSON

DANIEL PROTHEROE

Here comes that lit-tle black po-ny of mine, Gal-lop, a-gal-lop, a-gal-lop!__ His eyes are so bright and his coat is so fine, Gal-lop, a-gal-lop, a-gal-lop!__ His

The Lazy Cat

MOTHER GOOSE

J. W. ELLIOTT

Moderato

Pus - sy, where have you been to-day? In the mead-ows a - sleep in the hay?

Pus - sy, you are a la - zy cat, If you have done no more than that.

The Monkey

MAY MORGAN

PAUL AMBROSE

Moderato *

The mon-keys hang by hands or tails, Or swing from tree to tree; Per -

haps I look as strange to them, As mon - keys look to me.

*Children sing upper notes throughout. Teacher may sing the counter-melody.

The Circus

ANNA M. PRATT

EDWARD A. MUELLER

In marching tempo

Lit - tle John and Ben-nie and Bub, Heard the drums go rub-a-dub-dub;

Spoken
(rub-a-dub-dub) Off they went and saw in the tent Cir - cus hors-es danc-ing on a tub.

Circus Parade
(for dramatization)

EDWARD A. MUELLER

* The marchers here should stoop forward, keeping the knees bent, heads held low and wagging from side to side with each step, (two in a bar).

507514

poco a poco crescendo

con fuoco

D.S. with 2nd ending to Fine then to Trio

sfz   *sfz*   *sffz*

Trio
*The Ponies**

r.h. *r.h.* *r.h.* *r.h.*

Whoa!

D.C. to Fine

*A trotting step, lifting the knees high, one step to each beat.

The Black Thief

SARAH GRAMES CLARK

W. OTTO MIESSNER

There's trou-ble in the barn-yard, That I know; Just
You can't guess what's the mat-ter, That old crow

hear the hens a-cluck-ing And roost-ers crow!
up the chick-ens' break-fast; That I know!

The Duck and the Hen

RALPH CLARK Jr.

RUSSIAN FOLK SONG

Up-on the wa-ter swam a duck, "Quack, quack, quack," said the duck. Upon the shore a hen said, "cluck, Cluck, cluck," the hen said, "cluck."

Taddy Pole and Polly Wog

OLD NURSERY RHYME

MABEL E. BRAY

Tad-dy Pole and Pol-ly Wog Lived to-geth-er in a bog;
We might see the ver-y pool, Where they went to swim-ming school.

Three Little Kittens

TRADITIONAL TEXT

ENGLISH NURSERY DITTY

Moderato

1. There were three lit - tle kit - tens, Put on their mit - tens, To
2. These three lit - tle kit - tens, They lost their mit - tens, And
3. The three lit - tle kit - tens, They found their mit - tens, And

eat some Christ - mas pie.
all be - gan to sigh.
joy - ful - ly they did cry.

Mew, mew, mew, mew, mew, mew, mew.

The Little Red Hen

TRADITIONAL

W. OTTO MIESSNER

Moderato

Hen   Pig   Cat   Dog

1. Who will plant the seed?_____ "Not I!" "Not I!" "Not I!"
2. Who will cut the wheat?_____ "Not I!" "Not I!" "Not I!"
3. Who will thresh the wheat?_____ "Not I!" "Not I!" "Not I!"
4. Who will grind the wheat?_____ "Not I!" "Not I!" "Not I!"
5. Who will make the bread?_____ "Not I!" "Not I!" "Not I!"
6. Who will eat the bread?_____ "Oh I!" "Oh I!" "Oh I!"

Hen   All   *Ending for first five verses* *Ending for the last verse*

"I will plant the seed?_____ And she did!
"I will cut the wheat?_____ And she did!
"I will thresh the wheat?_____ And she did!
"I will grind the wheat?_____ And she did!
"I will make the bread?_____ And she did!
"I will eat the bread?_____ And she   did!

Mooley Cow Red

VIRGINIA BAKER

L. LESLIE LOTH

Moderato

Moo - ley Cow red, I'm lit - tle Ned, Please give me sweet milk To eat with my bread.

The Cat and the Dog

OLD NURSERY RHYME

MABEL E. BRAY

Quickly

Poor Dog Bright, ran off with all his might, Be-
Poor Cat Fright, ran off with all her might, Be-

cause the Cat was af - ter him. Poor Dog Bright!
cause the Dog was af - ter her. Poor Cat Fright!

Piggy-wig and Piggy-wee

W. OTTO MIESSNER

W. OTTO MIESSNER

Moderato

Pig - gy - - wig, and Pig - gy - wee, Live out

doors as you may see, And they nev - er seem to mind a - bout the

weath - er; But you ought to hear them squeal, When I

call them for a meal, These two lit - tle pigs to - geth - er.

The Young Engineer

MAY MORGAN

FRENCH FOLK SONG

I'm going to be an en-gi-neer And run a rail-way train, Through tun-nels, o-ver bridg-es, Up hill and down a-gain, I'll run the rail-way train.

The Flagman

MABEL E. BRAY

MABEL E. BRAY

A flag-man at the cross-ing, An au-to com-ing fast; The driv-er stops his mo-tor, Un-til the train is past.

The Fire

MABEL E. BRAY

OLD NURSERY GAME

Fire, fire, fire! See the en-gine go-ing!
Clang, clang, clang! Tell me what is burn-ing?
Shriek, shriek, shriek! All the si-rens blow-ing!
Dang, dang, dang! En-gines are re-turn-ing.

The Trolley Car

SARAH GRAMES CLARK

G. A. GRANT-SCHAEFER

Con moto
mf

On shin-y tracks the trol-ley cars Run hap-pi-ly a-long, And
The peo-ple come with shin-y coins And put them in the box, Then

up in front the trol-ley man Rings loud-ly at a gong.
set-tle down on shin-y seats To ride through cit-y blocks.

The Auto

NINA B. HARTFORD

NINA B HARTFORD

Brightly

Come,— climb in the au-to, We're off for the day, Far a-
Hear the au-to's big en-gine, It's hum-ming in-side, I am

way in the coun-try We will pic-nic and play.
sure it is hap-py When it takes us to ride.

The Airplane

MABEL E. BRAY

MABEL E. BRAY

Moderato

I like to watch the air-plane Go sail-ing thro' the sky;___ It

hums a song and skims a-long; I wish that I could fly!___

Buy

MOTHER GOOSE
Allegretto

RUSSIAN FOLK SONG

Smil-ing girls and ros-y boys, Come and buy my pret-ty
toys! Mon-keys made of gin-ger-bread, Sug-ar hors-es paint-ed red!

The Postman's Whistle

VERNETTA F. DECKER

EDWARD B. BIRGE

Brightly

The post-man blows his whis-tle And brings the mail to
you, I want to be a post-man; I have a whis-tle too!

The Postman

BLANCHE JENNINGS THOMPSON

PAUL AMBROSE

Quickly

Here comes the post-man, Run to the door;
Some-times there's one let-ter And some-times more.

In the Park

ANNA M. SHEPARD

GEOFFREY O'HARA

Gracefully

Trees a - bove our heads, Grass be - neath our feet,

Bench - es where the peo - ple sit To watch the pi - geons eat.

The Forge

RICHARD WAGNER
from "Siegfried"

Allegro moderato

p

staccato

The Fountain

ROSE FYLEMAN

OSBOURNE McCONATHY

Gracefully

Up - on the ter - race where I play, A lit - tle foun - tain sings all day A ti - ny tune;— It

leaps and pranc - es in the air; I saw a lit - tle fair - y there, This aft - er - noon.—

The Traffic Light

MABEL E. BRAY

PAUL AMBROSE

Brightly

The traf-fic light is red, We must not go a - head; But when the green is show-ing, Our
au - to will be go-ing. The traf-fic light is red, We must not go a - head.

The Traffic Cop

MABEL E. BRAY

DANIEL PROTHEROE

Moderato
mf

I like to see the traf-fic cop! I like to see him stand____ And
show the peo-ple where to go, By mov-ing just his hand.
cresc.

The Carpenters

NINA B. HARTFORD

NINA B. HARTFORD

Brightly

1. We are saw-ing our boards to-day; Saw, saw, saw, saw!
2. Now we ham-mer and pound a - way; Pound, pound, pound, pound!
3. Up the lad-der we climb so high; Climb, climb, climb, climb!

We are saw-ing our boards to-day; Car-pen-ters all are we.
Now we ham-mer and pound a - way; Car-pen-ters all are we.
Up the lad-der we climb so high; Car-pen-ters all are we.

I am the Wind

MARY W. RAYMOND

PAUL AMBROSE

I am the wind, and I come ver-y fast; Oo___ Oo___ Oo!___

Through the wood I blow a blast,___ Oo___ Oo___ Oo!___

Murmuring Zephyrs
(Swaying in the Breeze)

ADOLF JENSEN

The Storm

MABEL E. BRAY

GEORGE LeROY LINDSAY

How it blows and storms and pours! Rain is fall-ing fast. Hur-ry in and shut the doors, 'Till the storm is past. *R.H.*

Old Mother Wind

CHINESE MOTHER GOOSE RHYME

HARRIET WARE

Old Moth-er Wind,— Come this way, And make our ba-by Cool to-day. Oo._____ Oo._____

Moonlight

VERNETTA F. DECKER

EDWARD B. BIRGE

When the moon is big and bright, It makes the bed-room floor look white; And out-side where the tall trees grow, It makes the ground look white as snow.

The Sun

BLANCHE JENNINGS THOMPSON

PAUL AMBROSE

Brightly

When the sun gets up in the morn - ing And combs his gold - en hair, __ I

get my ball and roll - er skates, For I know it will be fair. When the

sun gets up in the morn - ing And goes right back to bed, I

get my boots and rain - coat out, For I know 'twill rain __ in - stead. __

The Wishing Star

AGNES CHOATE WONSON

W. OTTO MIESSNER

Quietly

pp

Star - - light, Star - - bright, First

star I've seen to - night! How I wish you'd come to play

Down __ here with me, Some day! __

Ped. *

Rainy Day

MABEL E. BRAY

L. LESLIE LOTH

Moderato

Rain - y day! Rain - y day! Fields are wet and the skies are gray.

Drip - ping down, drip - ping down, Rain is drop-ping on all the town.

Little Raindrops

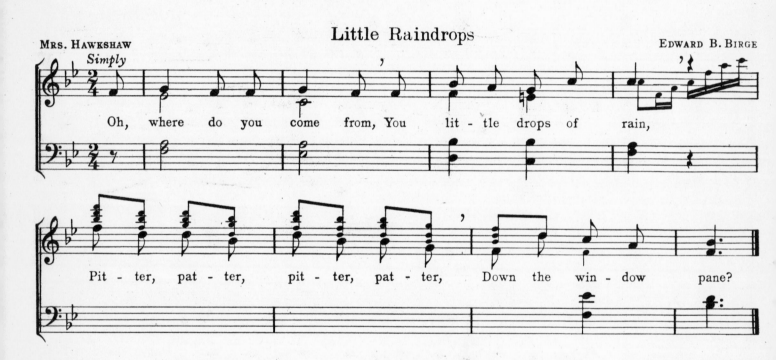

MRS. HAWKSHAW

EDWARD B. BIRGE

Simply

Oh, where do you come from, You lit - tle drops of rain,

Pit - ter, pat - ter, pit - ter, pat - ter, Down the win - dow pane?

The Brook

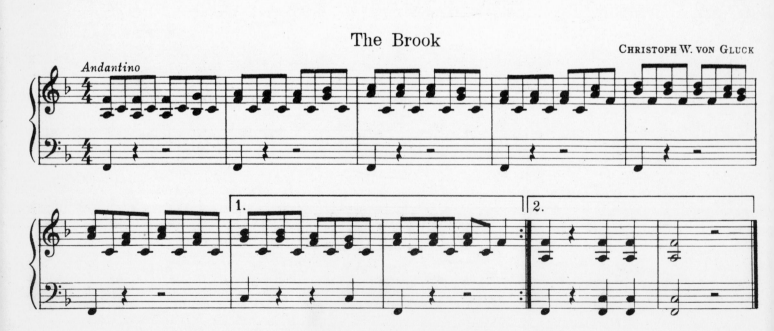

CHRISTOPH W. VON GLUCK

Andantino

Boats Sail on the Rivers

Christina Rossetti

French Nursery Song

Boats sail on the riv - ers, And ships sail on the seas; ____ But
clouds that sail a - cross the sky Are pret - tier far than these. ____

At the Seaside

Robert Louis Stevenson

W. Otto Miessner

When I was down be - side the sea, A wood - en spade they
My holes were emp - ty like a cup, In ev - 'ry hole the

gave to me, To dig the sand - y shore, To dig the sand - y shore.
sea came up Till it could come no more, Till it could come no more.

The Lake

William Sterndale Bennett

The Mountain

Anna M. Shepard

Geoffrey O'Hara

Broadly

The beau-ti-ful moun-tain ris-es high Like a might-y gi-ant a-gainst the sky.

In the Wood

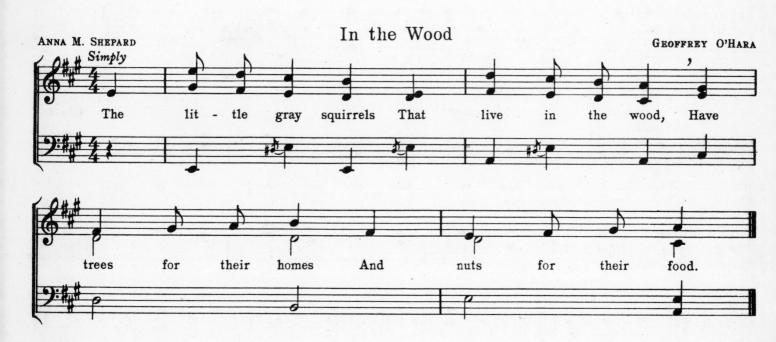

Anna M. Shepard

Geoffrey O'Hara

Simply

The lit-tle gray squirrels That live in the wood, Have

trees for their homes And nuts for their food.

Theme from the Sonata in A
(Swaying trees)

Wolfgang Amadeus Mozart

Gracefully

I Wish

BLANCHE JENNINGS THOMPSON*

G. A. GRANT-SCHAEFER

Allegretto

I wish I were a fair - y With sil - ver wings that shine; ____ It

must be fun to spread them out And think, "These wings are mine!" ____

* From THE GOLDEN TRUMPETS by Blanche Jennings Thompson. By permission of The Macmillan Company, publishers.

The Little Goblin

BLANCHE JENNINGS THOMPSON*

EDWARD B. BIRGE

Mysteriously

See the lit - tle Gob - lin, With his coat of leath - er,

Wear - ing in his ti - ny cap, A long black feath - er.

* From THE GOLDEN TRUMPETS by Blanche Jennings Thompson. By permission of The Macmillan Company, publishers.

Brownies

BLANCHE JENNINGS THOMPSON

DANIEL PROTHEROE

Moderato

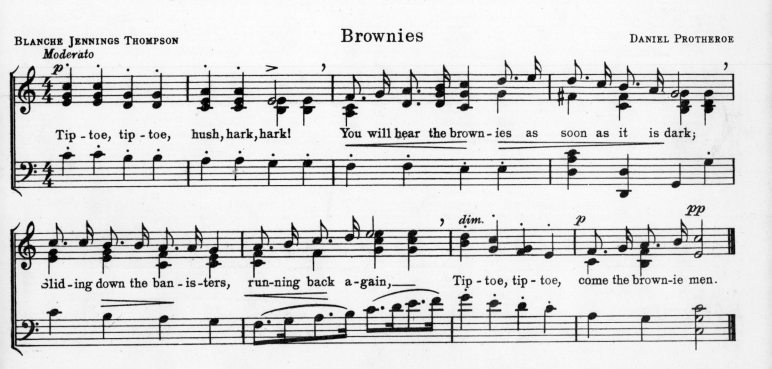

Tip - toe, tip - toe, hush, hark, hark! You will hear the brown - ies as soon as it is dark;

Slid - ing down the ban - is - ters, run - ning back a - gain, ____ Tip - toe, tip - toe, come the brown - ie men.

Moonlight Scene from "One Thousand and One Nights"
(Fairies in moonlight)

CARL REINECKE

BLANCHE JENNINGS THOMPSON*

The Dragon

G. A. GRANT-SCHAEFER

Did you ev-er see a drag-on? He's a ver-y fear-some beast.
On __ fire and smoke and burn-ing coals He likes to sit and feast.

He __ has a long and shin-ing tail; His claws are sharp and bright, I __

should-n't like to meet one in the dusk-y woods at night.

* From THE GOLDEN TRUMPETS by Blanche Jennings Thompson. By permission of The Macmillan Company, publishers.

Fairies' March

FELIX MENDELSSOHN
From "Midsummer Night's Dream"

Da Capo al 𝄋

After Da Capo, skip from 𝄋 to ⊕

The Giants

RICHARD WAGNER
From "Rheingold"

Entr'acte Music
(Quiet Fairies)

FRANZ SCHUBERT
From "Rosamunde"

Stephanie Gavotte
(Fairies' Dance)

ALPHONS CZIBULKA

Album Leaf
(Brownies' March)

EDVARD GRIEG

Play this part twice, then a third time as far as Fine

"Minute" Waltz
(Happy Fairies)

FAIRY WORLD

FREDERIC CHOPIN

Nocturne
(Fairies Asleep)

FELIX MENDELSSOHN
From "Midsummer Night's Dream"

Foreboding of Grief
(Sad Fairies)

ROBERT SCHUMANN

Larghetto
(Goblins)

ROBERT SCHUMANN

X. CYCLE OF SEASONS

(A.) AUTUMN

The Four Seasons

Anna M. Shepard

Geoffrey O'Hara

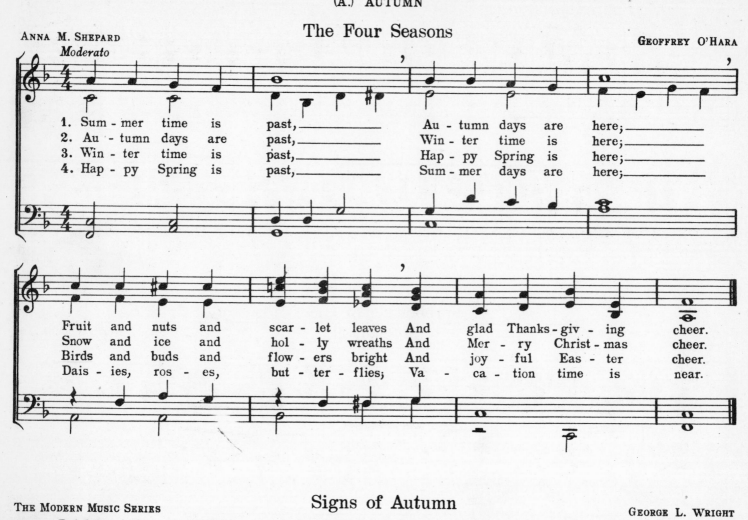

1. Sum-mer time is past,_____ Au-tumn days are here;_____
2. Au-tumn days are past,_____ Win-ter time is here;_____
3. Win-ter time is past,_____ Hap-py Spring is here;_____
4. Hap-py Spring is past,_____ Sum-mer days are here;_____

Fruit and nuts and scar-let leaves And glad Thanks-giv-ing cheer.
Snow and ice and hol-ly wreaths And Mer-ry Christ-mas cheer.
Birds and buds and flow-ers bright And joy-ful Eas-ter cheer.
Dais-ies, ros-es, but-ter-flies; Va-ca-tion time is near.

Signs of Autumn

The Modern Music Series

George L. Wright

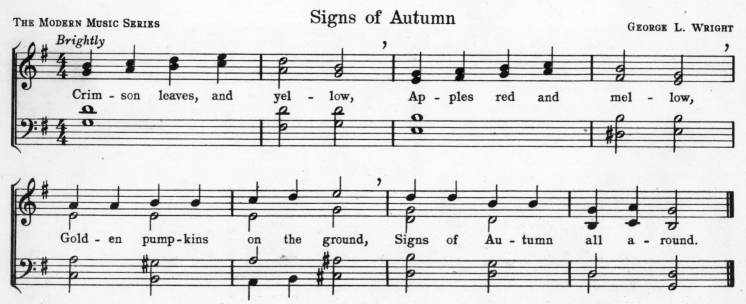

Crim-son leaves, and yel-low, Ap-ples red and mel-low,

Gold-en pump-kins on the ground, Signs of Au-tumn all a-round.

Fluttering Leaves

Nina B. Hartford

Nina B. Hartford

Red,____ or-ange, gold and brown,____ Au-tumn leaves come flut-ter-ing down.____

Valse
(Dancing Leaves)

FREDERIC CHOPIN
(Simplified)

D. C. al Fine

The Crow

NINA B. HARTFORD

NINA B. HARTFORD

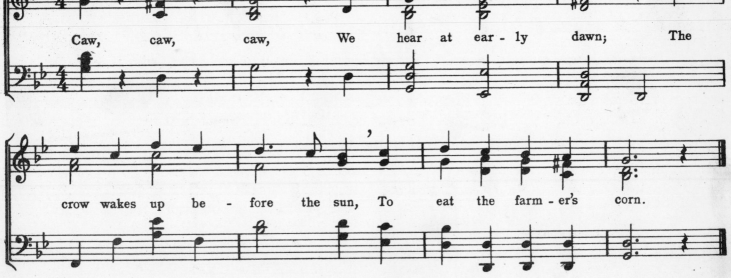

Caw, caw, caw, We hear at ear - ly dawn; The crow wakes up be - fore the sun, To eat the farm - er's corn.

Melody
(Fall Things Blowing)

FELIX MENDELSSOHN

Caprice
(Birds Fly Away)

CHRISTOPH W. VON GLUCK
From "Alceste"

November

Anonymous   EDWARD B. BIRGE

Trees __ bare and brown, ___ Dry leaves ev - 'ry - where,
Red-cheek'd ap - ples roast - ed, Pop - corn al - most done,

Danc - ing up and down, ___ Whirl - ing through the air.
Toes and chest - nuts toast - ed, That's No - vem - ber fun.

(B.) WINTER

Which Way Does the Wind Blow?

LUCY AIKIN

GERMAN FOLK SONG

Moderato

Which way does the wind blow? And where does he go? He rides o'er the wa-ter And o-ver the snow.

Snowbirds

MABEL E. BRAY

RUSSIAN FOLK SONG

Slowly

Man-y birds have gone a-way, Fly-ing to the south to stay.

I am glad you do not go E-ven when there's ice and snow.

January

SARA COLERIDGE

GERMAN FOLK SONG

Moderato

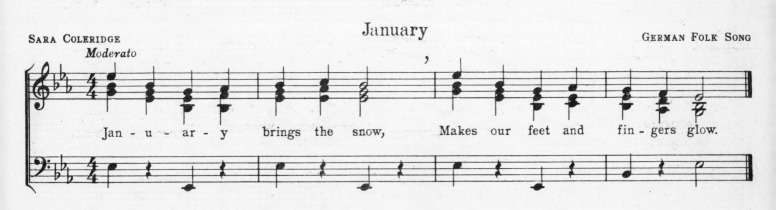

Jan-u-ar-y brings the snow, Makes our feet and fin-gers glow.

The Poor Snow-Man

Vernetta F. Decker

Edward B. Birge

The Snow-man has-n't an-y bed,_____ He does-n't sleep, you know;_____ But

out-doors must be ver-y cold_____ When you're all made of snow!

Mazurka Russe
(Snowballing)

Louis Ganne

Melody marcato

* If desired, the part for left hand may be omitted.

Snowflakes

George L. Wright

Delicately

Making a Snow-Man

SARAH GRAMES CLARK

HARRIET WARE

Allegretto

If you would make a snow-man, Put on your warm-est dress, Your mit-tens and your
wool-ey coat, Your muff-ler, too, I guess. And don't for-get your leg-gins, What-
ev-er else you do, For gay Jack Frost and bold North Wind Will be out-doors with you!

rit.

Coasting

NINA B. HARTFORD

NINA B. HARTFORD

Moderato

Coast - ing, coast - ing, Down the hill we go; Oh
Coast - ing, coast - ing, Tum - bling now and then, With

win - ter brings the great - est fun, With ice and drift - ing snow.
laugh and shout we turn a - bout And climb the hill a - gain.

Spring Song

FELIX MENDELSSOHN
From "Songs Without Words"

Allegretto grazioso

Melody in F
(Spring Mood)

ANTON RUBINSTEIN

Moderato

Spring Song

GEORGE E. THOMPSON, Jr.
JAMES H. ROGERS

Smoothly, in moderate waltz time

A bird sails, and a cloud sails, And the sun shines down so bright.— The tu-lips and the daf-fo-dils Are a ver-y pret-ty sight.—

Beginning To Grow

ANNETTE WYNNE
ANICE TERHUNE

Softly and blithely

A fair-y wakes and starts to sing, The grass-es hear be-low; And ev-'ry seed says "Why, it's spring, I guess I'll have to grow!"

Reprinted by permission from "For Days and Days," A Year-round Treasury of Verse for Children, by Annette Wynne.
Copyright, 1919, by Frederick A. Stokes Company.

Fly, Kite

BLANCHE JENNINGS THOMPSON
MABEL E. BRAY

Slowly

Fly, kite, fly!— So high, so high. Sail a-bove the pas-tures;
Fly, kite, fly!— Fly, kite, fly! So high, so high!—

The Baby Leaves

SARAH GRAMES CLARK

PAUL AMBROSE

Wake, ba-by leaves, for Spring-time is call-ing you! Soft are the breez-es and bright the sun;

Wake, ba-by leaves, for Spring-time has come; Wake, ba-by leaves, for Spring-time has come!

Baby Buds

Anonymous

EDWARD B. BIRGE

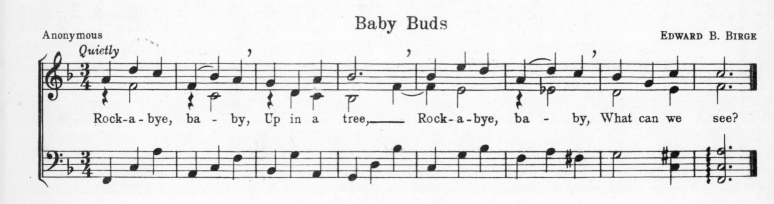

Rock-a-bye, ba-by, Up in a tree,___ Rock-a-bye, ba-by, What can we see?

April Rain

AGNES CHOATE WONSON

W. OTTO MIESSNER

A-pril, A-pril, Why do you cry___ All these tear-drops down from the sky?___

Don't you know your lit-tle show'rs Are ti-ny drinks for thirst-y___ flow'rs?

Summer Days

NINA B. HARTFORD   NINA B. HARTFORD

When days in sum-mer are hot and dry, With not a cool-ing
The birds sing gai-ly in branch-es high, The air is cool and

breeze, _____ We take our lunch to the shad-y woods And
sweet, _____ But best of all is the rip-pling brook Where

rest be-neath the trees, _____ Be-neath the whisp-'ring trees. _____
we may splash our feet, _____ We wade and splash our feet. _____

Invitation to the Dance

CARL M. von WEBER

Summer Night

SIR HENRY NEWBOLT

G. A. GRANT-SCHAEFER

Lento

Night is come, Owls are out, Bee - tles hum Round a -

bout. Night is come, Owls are out, Bee - tles hum Round a - bout.

Boating Song

GEORGE S. APPLEGARTH

THE MODERN MUSIC SERIES

In the tempo of rowing

Row - ing,____ row - ing,____ Gen - tly the wa - ter is flow - ing, flow - ing.
Plash - ing,____ plash - ing,____ Oars in the wa - ter are splash - ing, splash - ing.

Row - ing,____ row - ing,____ O - ver the riv - er we're go - - ing.
Plash - ing,____ plash - ing,____ Bright - ly the rip - ples are flash - - ing.

Tap, Tap, Tap!

SARAH GRAMES CLARK

L. LESLIE LOTH

Happily

Tap, tap, tap! Tap, tap, tap! I know who knocks like that!_____ The

old wood - peck - er in - vit - ing you To see his new red hat!

Thirsty Butterfly

Ella D. Watkins

Anice Terhune

A tu - lip lifts its pret - ty cup, Then rain-drops come and fill it up. A

but - ter - fly now takes a drink, Which makes the tu - lip glad, I think.

The Cherry Tree

Ella D. Watkins

Harriet Ware

One morn - ing, not so long a - go, The cher - ry tree was white as snow. It

now has changed from white to green, With ripe, red cher - ries in be - tween.

Beds

Florence C. Fox

G. A. Grant-Schaefer

Ba - by sleeps in a cra - dle, Bird - ie sleeps in a tree,___ The

dor - mouse sleeps in an un-der-ground house, And there's e - ven a bed for the bee.___

Columbus Was a Sailor

BLANCHE JENNINGS THOMPSON

DANIEL PROTHEROE

Allegretto

Co - lum - bus was a sail - or bold, A dar - ing man was he;____ He crossed the storm - y sea to find A - mer - i - ca for me.____

Hallowe'en Night

BLANCHE JENNINGS THOMPSON

ANICE TERHUNE

Lively

Witch - es ride on Hal - low - e'en, Ho! Ho! Ho!____ Their cloaks are black, their eyes are green, Oh! Oh! Oh!____ Ev - 'ry witch has a tall black hat, Ho! Ho! Ho!____ And ev - 'ry witch has a big black cat, Oh! Oh! Oh!__

Thanksgiving

ANNA M. SHEPARD

Broadly

GEOFFREY O'HARA

Sing a song of thank-ful-ness, For things that make us glad;____ For

friends we meet and things we eat, For moth-er, home and dad.

Christmas Chimes

OLD SONG

Moderato

OLD CHRISTMAS SONG

Ding, dong, ding, dong, Christ-mas com-ing! Hear the ring-ing chimes!____

Ding, dong, ding, dong, Christ-mas com-ing! Hap-pi-est of times!

Christmas Day

MABEL E. BRAY

Moderato

DANIEL PROTHEROE

Bells and drums and sol-diers tall,____ Dolls and en-gines, gifts for all,____

Hol-ly wreaths and rib-bons gay,____ Make a mer-ry Christ-mas Day.

A Christmas Song

VIRGINIA BAKER

OSBOURNE McCONATHY

Sing a song of Christ-mas, A cake full of plums, Four and twen-ty snow-birds To

pick up the crumbs; Stock-ings full of can-dy, Books and games and toys,

Is-n't it a mer-ry time For lit-tle girls and boys?

Kris Kringle's Travels

SUSIE M. BEST

G. A. GRANT-SCHAEFER

A jol-ly old fel-low is Mis-ter Kris Krin-gle; He's com-ing! He's com-ing! Just hear his bells jin-gle.

Dancing Doll
(Christmas Toys)

ED. POLDINI

Adeste Fideles
(Christmas Processional)

It is supposed that this hymn was written by John Reading, an English organist of the 18th century.

Nazareth
(For the Christmas Program)

CHARLES GOUNOD

Fine

D. C. al Fine

Silent Night

FRANZ GRUBER

Happy New Year

ANNA M. SHEPARD   G. A. GRANT-SCHAEFER

Hap-py New Year! Hap-py New Year! Let us say when we meet on New Year's Day. Hap-py New Year! Hap-py New Year! Let us say when we meet on New Year's Day.

Abraham Lincoln

MABEL E. BRAY   BUGLE CALL

Oh, Lin-coln! Oh, Lin-coln! To-day we sing of you.___ Oh, Lin-coln! Oh, Lin-coln! So no-ble, good, and true.___

George Washington's Birthday

MABEL E. BRAY   NAVY BUGLE CALL

Feb-ru-a-ry twen-ty-sec-ond! Wash-ing-ton we hon-or thee! Long a-go you made our coun-try Strong and hap-py, great and free.

Who'll Be My Valentine?

Vernetta F. Decker

Mabel E. Bray

Who will be my val-en-tine? O, I'll be yours, if you'll be mine. If

I may have a heart from you, This heart so red I'll give you, too.

Easter-Time

Anna M. Shepard

George L. Wright

East-er-time is here a-gain, Sun-shine bright or drip-ping rain,

Flow-ers in the earth so deep Wak-en from their win-ter sleep.

Arbor Day

Vernetta F. Decker

Daniel Protheroe

We plant a tree for Ar-bor Day, A ver-y lit-tle tree. The

rain and sun will make it grow To shel-ter you and me.

May Day

BLANCHE JENNINGS THOMPSON

EDWARD A. MUELLER

Twist a crown of May-flow'rs, Of May-flow'rs, Of May-flow'rs,

Twist a crown of May-flow'rs, To crown our queen to-day.

For Our Soldiers

VERNETTA F. DECKER

GEORGE LEROY LINDSAY

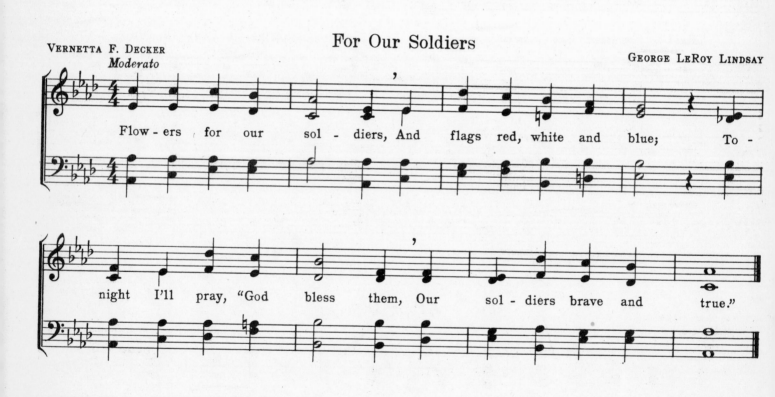

Flow-ers for our sol-diers, And flags red, white and blue; To-

night I'll pray, "God bless them, Our sol-diers brave and true."

Our Flag

MABEL E. BRAY

BUGLE CALL
From "General's March"

Hail to the flag! Wave it on high! Red, white and blue, Let it float to the sky!

Birthday Song

BLANCHE JENNINGS THOMPSON

DANIEL PROTHEROE

Hap-py Birth-day! Hap-py Birth-day! May the skies be blue, May the sun-shine fol-low you all the whole— year through.

Baby's Birthday

AGNES CHOATE WONSON

W. OTTO MIESSNER

Ba-by, see, a cake for you, It's your birth-day, you are two! Moth-er, will you cut a slice, If we both act grown-up and nice?

Little Jack Horner

MOTHER GOOSE   J. W. ELLIOTT

Allegretto con moto

Lit-tle Jack Hor - ner Sat in a cor - ner, Eat-ing a Christ - mas pie; _____ He

put in his thumb, And pull'd out a plum, And said,"What a good boy am I!"

Dickory, Dickory, Dock

MOTHER GOOSE   J. W. ELLIOTT

Allegro

Dick-o-ry, dick-o-ry, dock; The mouse ran up the clock; The

clock struck One, The mouse ran down; Dick-o-ry, dick-o-ry, dock.

Bobby Shafto

MOTHER GOOSE

W. OTTO MIESSNER

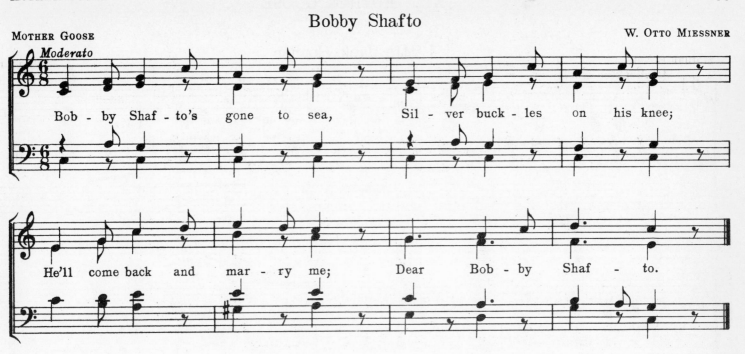

Bob - by Shaf - to's gone to sea, Sil - ver buck - les on his knee;

He'll come back and mar - ry me; Dear Bob - by Shaf - to.

A, B, C, tumble down D

MOTHER GOOSE

J. W. ELLIOTT

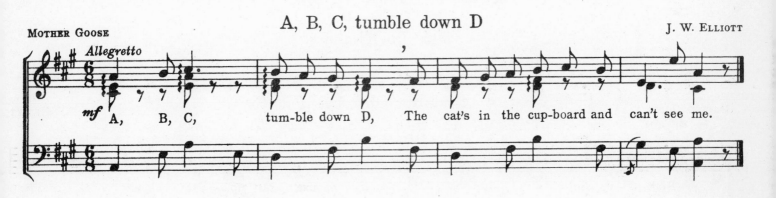

A, B, C, tum-ble down D, The cat's in the cup-board and can't see me.

See-saw, Margery Daw

MOTHER GOOSE

J. W. ELLIOTT

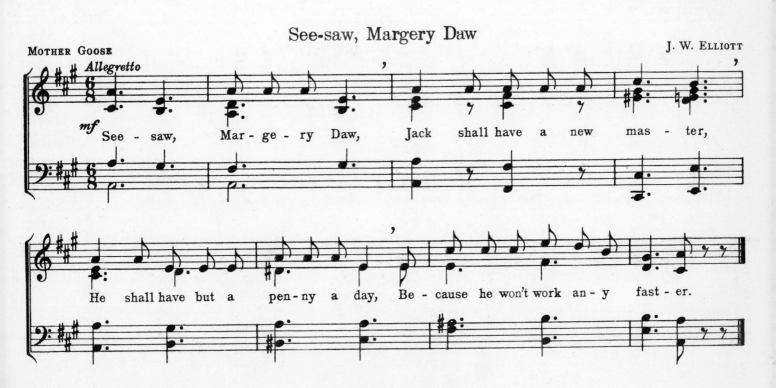

See - saw, Mar - ge - ry Daw, Jack shall have a new mas - ter,

He shall have but a pen-ny a day, Be - cause he won't work an - y fast - er.

Hey, Diddle Diddle

MOTHER GOOSE

J. W. ELLIOTT

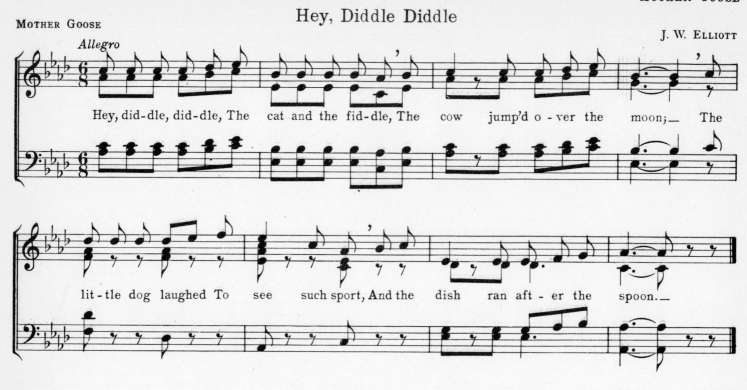

Hey, did-dle, did-dle, The cat and the fid-dle, The cow jump'd o-ver the moon;— The lit-tle dog laughed To see such sport, And the dish ran aft-er the spoon.—

Jack Be Nimble

MOTHER GOOSE

WILLIAM A. WHITE

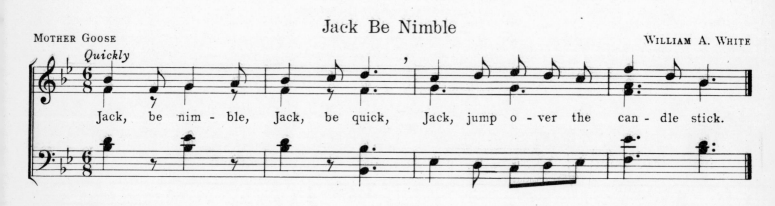

Jack, be nim - ble, Jack, be quick, Jack, jump o - ver the can - dle stick.

Little Miss Muffet

MOTHER GOOSE

EDITH AYERS McCULLOUGH

Lit-tle Miss Muf-fet Sat on a tuf-fet, Eat-ing some curds and whey,_____ There came a great spi-der and sat down be - side her, And fright-en'd Miss Muf-fet a - way._____

The Fair Land of Poland
(March)

MICHAEL BALFE
From "Bohemian Girl"

Pirates' March

ARTHUR SULLIVAN
From "Pirates of Penzance"

March

CARL M. von WEBER

Andante
(Lightly Stepping)

FRANZ JOSEPH HAYDN
From "Surprise Symphony"

Gipsy Rondo
(Running)

FRANZ JOSEPH HAYDN

March
(Running)

GEORGES BIZET
From "Carmen"

Allemande
(Jumping and Hopping)

FRANÇOIS COUPERIN

Variations on a French Melody
(Hopping and Jumping)

Wolfgang Amadeus Mozart

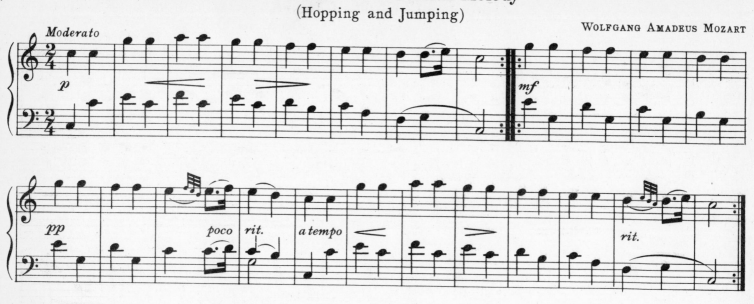

The Flatterer
(Butterfly)

Cecile Chaminade

Happy and Light of Heart
(Skipping)

MICHAEL BALFE
From "Bohemian Girl"

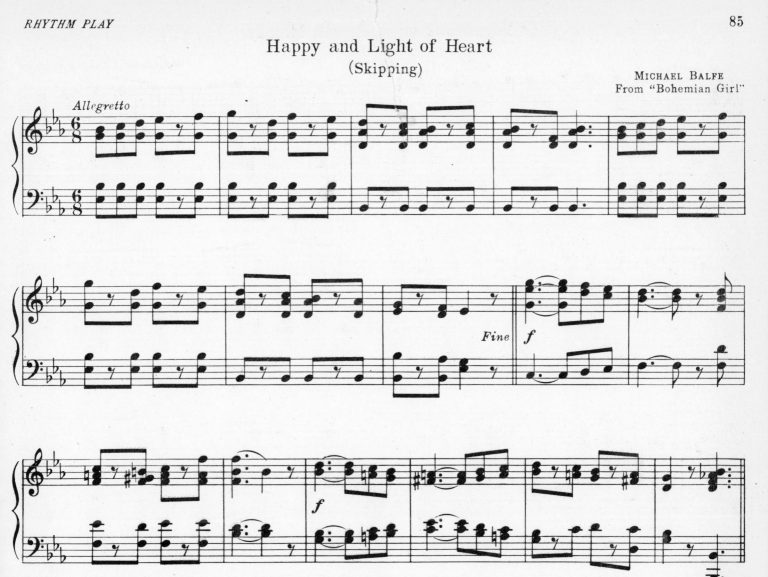

D.C. al Fine

Malbrough Has Gone to War
(Skipping)

ANCIENT CRUSADERS' SONG

D.C. al Fine

The Wild Rider

(Galloping)

ROBERT SCHUMANN

XIV. TOY ORCHESTRA

Finale from Sonata in D

Franz Joseph Haydn

* See page 195

D.C.

Minuet

Wolfgang Amadeus Mozart
From "Don Juan"

Little Minuet in G

Johann Sebastian Bach

Gavotte

George Frederick Handel

Original Version

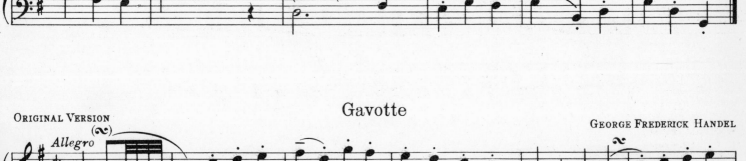

Gavotte in D

NICOLAI von WILM

Toreador Song

GEORGES BIZET
From "Carmen"

Cradle Song

Nicolai von Wilm

Turkish March

Ludwig van Beethoven

XV. MOODS
(To be played for the children)

Cradle Song

ROBERT SCHUMANN

Evening Prayer

ENGELBERT HUMPERDINCK
From "Hansel and Gretel"

O Tender Moon

Charles Gounod
From "Faust"

Larghetto

_mf_

Boat Song

Charles Gounod

Andante

> _dolce_

_p_

mf cre - scen - do

rall.

Habanera

GEORGES BIZET
From "Carmen"

Gavotte

OLD FRENCH

Minuet

OLD FRENCH

Cradle Song

MISKA HAUSER

Largo

GEORGE FREDERICK HANDEL
From "Xerxes"

Waltz, № 2

JOHANNES BRAHMS

Don Baltazar Carlos on Horseback, Velasquez (1599-1660)

PART TWO
The First Grade

I. AROUND THE HOME

My Baby-Bo

Laura E. Richards

W. Otto Miessner

Fly a-way, Bird-ie, oh! Bring some-thing home to my Ba-by-Bo; Bring her a feath-er and bring her a song, Sing to her sweet-ly the whole day long.

Rockaway Land

Edith L. Bokeloh

Edward B. Birge

O, Rock-a-way land is the land of dreams, And moth-er's arms point the way;___ The pleas-ant-est place of all it seems, Aft-er the hours of play.___

Mother and Father

MABEL E. BRAY

MABEL E. BRAY

Simply

Moth - er is the dear - est Of all the friends I know;_____ She
Fa - ther is the kind - est Of all the friends I know;_____ He

helps me work and helps me play; That's why I love her so._____
likes to take me out with him; That's why I love him so._____

Baby's Lullaby

SAMUEL BURNHAM

H. E. HOLT

Quietly

Lull - a - by, lull - a - by, Ba - by must sleep. Now when the day - light dies,
Lull - a - by, lull - a - by, Ba - by must sleep. Moth - er will watch and pray,

Closed be the lit - tle eyes; Rest till the sun a - rise. Sleep, ba - by, sleep.
Dan - ger may keep a - way, Un - til the dawn of day. Sleep, ba - by, sleep.

Ann's Teeth

WALTER DE LA MARE

W. OTTO MIESSNER

Brightly

Now twelve a - bove, And twice six be - neath, She must pol - ish and

pol - ish her small_____ white_____ teeth._____

The Land of Counterpane

ROBERT LOUIS STEVENSON

W. OTTO MIESSNER

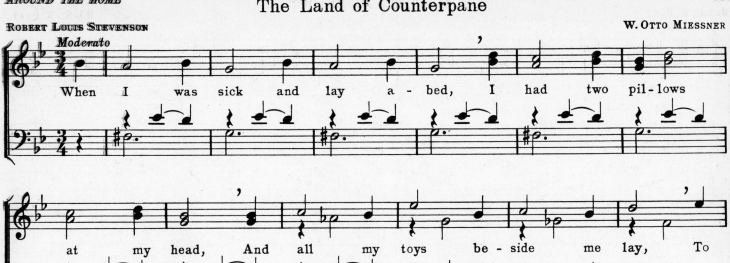

When I was sick and lay a-bed, I had two pil-lows at my head, And all my toys be-side me lay, To keep me hap-py all the day.

Cradle Time

AGNES CHOATE WONSON

W. OTTO MIESSNER

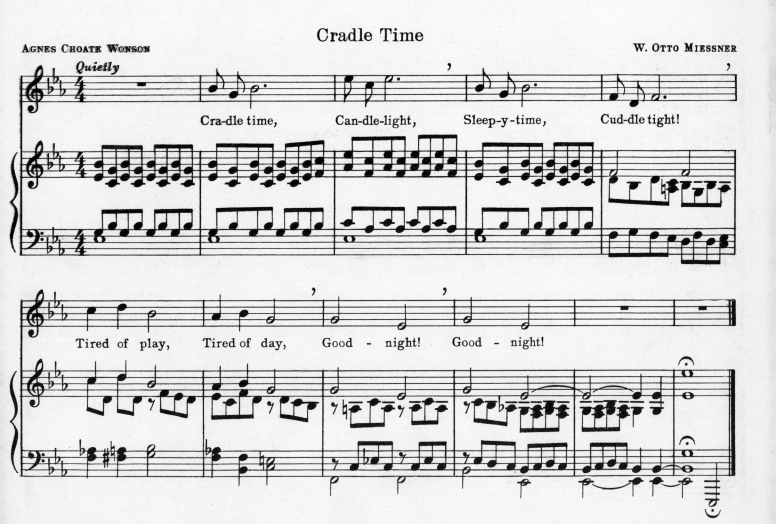

Cra-dle time, Can-dle-light, Sleep-y-time, Cud-dle tight!

Tired of play, Tired of day, Good-night! Good-night!

Mix a Pancake

Christina Rossetti

Mildred Hinkle Halle

With spirit

Mix a pan-cake, Stir a pan-cake, Pop it in the pan;

Fry the pan-cake, Toss the pan-cake, Catch it if you can.

Housekeeping

Old Nursery Rhyme

Old Nursery Song

Brightly

1. Mon - day is the day for wash - ing, Wash - ing, wash - ing,
2. Tues - day is the day for iron - ing, Iron - ing, iron - ing,
3. Wednes - day is the day for mend - ing, Mend - ing, mend - ing,
4. Thurs - day is the day for clean - ing, Clean - ing, clean - ing,
5. Fri - day is the day for call - ing, Call - ing, call - ing,
6. Sat - ur - day we do the bak - ing, Bak - ing, bak - ing,

Mon - day is the day for wash - ing, For wash - ing the clothes.
Tues - day is the day for iron - ing, For iron - ing the clothes.
Wednes - day is the day for mend - ing, For mend - ing the clothes.
Thurs - day is the day for clean - ing, For clean - ing the house.
Fri - day is the day for call - ing, For meet - ing our friends.
Sat - ur - day we do the bak - ing, The bread and the pies.

When Daddy Comes Home

GEORGE S. APPLEGARTH
W. OTTO MIESSNER

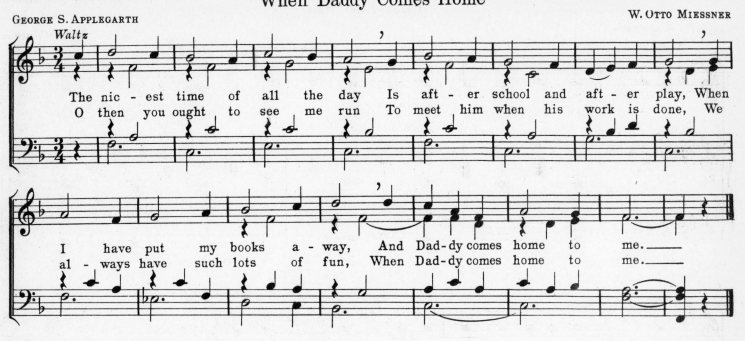

The nic - est time of all the day Is aft - er school and aft - er play, When
O then you ought to see me run To meet him when his work is done, We

I have put my books a - way, And Dad-dy comes home to me.____
al - ways have such lots of fun, When Dad-dy comes home to me.____

Friends For Tea

MABEL E. BRAY
MABEL E. BRAY

When peo - ple come to our house To have a cup of tea.____

____ I al - ways sit up tall and straight, As good as good can be.____

Callers

VERNETTA F. DECKER
EDWARD B. BIRGE

I peeped in - to the par-lor door, And there a la - dy sat;____ She

had a love - ly pock-et book, And wore a pret - ty hat.

Work and Play

CHRISTINA ROSSETTI

HARRIET WARE

A pock-et hand-ker-chief to hem, Oh, dear, Oh! dear, Oh! dear! For man-y stitch-es it will take un-til it's done, I fear. But set a stitch and then a stitch, And stitch and stitch a-way, Till stitch by stitch the hem is done; And aft-er work is play. A pock-et hand-ker-chief to hem, Oh, dear, Oh! dear, Oh! dear!

Good Night

LORD HOUGHTON

PAUL AMBROSE

Simply

A fair lit-tle girl sat un-der a tree, Sew-ing as long as her eyes could see; Then smoothed out her work and fold-ed it right, And said, "Dear work, Good night, good night." And said, "Dear work, Good night, good night!"

Come, Let's to Bed

MOTHER GOOSE

W. A. WHITE

Moderato

Come, let's to bed, says Sleep-y Head; Tar-ry a while, says Slow; Put on the pan, says Greed-y Nan, Let's sup be-fore we go.

The Looking-Glass Child

NINA B. HARTFORD

NINA B. HARTFORD

Brightly

The child in the mir-ror I love to see; I smile at her and she smiles at me.

Bed Time

NINA B. HARTFORD

NINA B. HARTFORD

When the day is done, and the gold-en sun In the west is round and red; Then he seems to say, "You must stop your play, For it's time to go to bed."

A Happy Child

KATE GREENAWAY

EDWARD B. BIRGE

My house is red—a lit-tle house; A hap-py child am I; I laugh and play the live-long day; I hard-ly ev-er cry.

Gray Pony

NINA B. HARTFORD

NINA B. HARTFORD

Come on, Gray Po-ny, let's gal-lop a-way, The sky is blue, it's a beau-ti-ful day; We'll cross the mead-ow, the hill and plain; Then turn a-bout, Po-ny, and home a-gain;

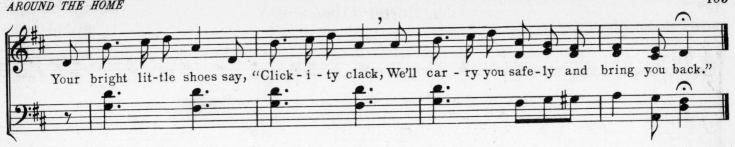

Your bright lit-tle shoes say, "Click-i-ty clack, We'll car-ry you safe-ly and bring you back."

My Dicky Bird

MABEL L. HARRIS

Brightly

IRENE R. BRICKNER

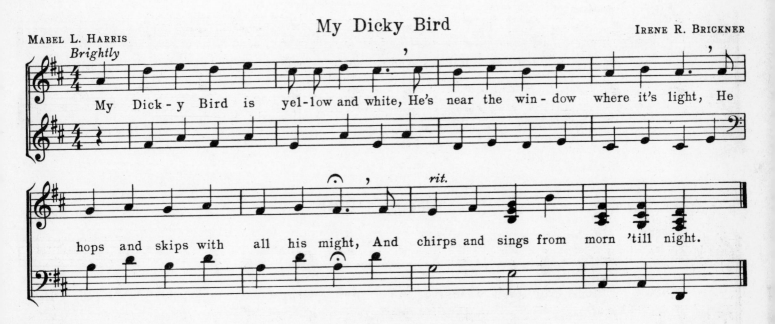

My Dick-y Bird is yel-low and white, He's near the win-dow where it's light, He hops and skips with all his might, And chirps and sings from morn 'till night.

When Cats Get Up

NURSERY RHYME

Brightly

FRENCH FOLK SONG

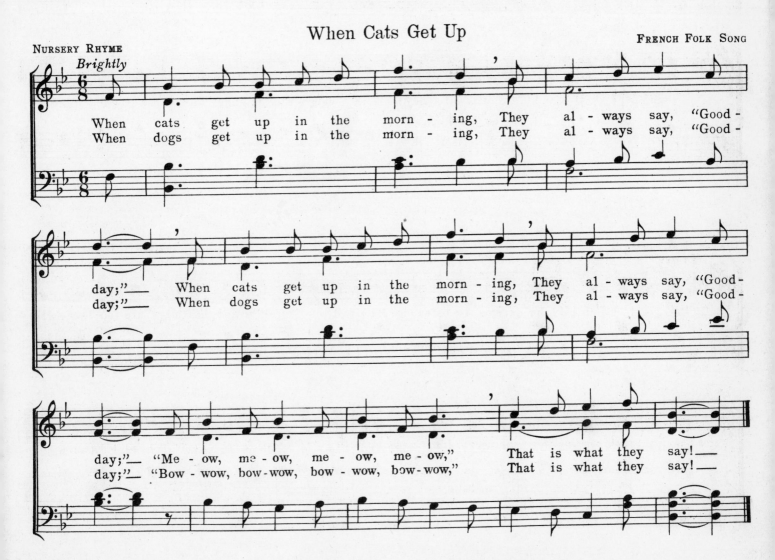

When cats get up in the morn-ing, They al-ways say, "Good-
When dogs get up in the morn-ing, They al-ways say, "Good-

day;"___ When cats get up in the morn-ing, They al-ways say, "Good-
day;"___ When dogs get up in the morn-ing, They al-ways say, "Good-

day;"___ "Me-ow, me-ow, me-ow, me-ow," That is what they say!___
day;"___ "Bow-wow, bow-wow, bow-wow, bow-wow," That is what they say!___

Oh, Here is Miss Pussy

From CHILD LIFE IN SONG

HORATIO PARKER

Gently

Oh, here is Miss Pus-sy, She's drink-ing her milk;___ Her
coat is as soft And as gloss-y as silk.

Doggie's Bath

E. GORDON BROWNE

PAUL AMBROSE

Briskly

Now I must fill the wash-ing tub And give my darl-ing dog a scrub, He's
scam-per'd up and down all day; With dog-gie friends he loves to play.

Funny Little Bunny

GEORGE S. APPLEGARTH

L. LESLIE LOTH

Not quickly

Lit-tle Jack Rab-bit, he seems to be wrong; His tail is so short and his ears are so long, His
front legs are weak and his hind legs are strong, And hip-pi-ty-hop he goes bob-bing a-long.

The Telephone

NINA B. HARTFORD

NINA B. HARTFORD

*Hel-lo, — Hel-lo, And how are you to-day? We're
Hel-lo, Hel-lo, We'll be there right a-way; We're

ver-y well, we thank you; Can you come out to play? We're
glad you're com-ing o-ver, We'll have a hap-py day.

*Roman type — Boys sing
Italics ——— Girls sing
Last phrase — All sing

The Fireman

LINN MOORE MILLER

LINN MOORE MILLER
With vigor

Cling, clang, cling, Cling, clang, cling, Cling, cling, cling, cling, Cling, cling, cling; The

fire-man with the en-gine goes, With lad-ders and the big, big, hose.

Splash-ing, dash-ing all a-bout, And soon the fire is out, And soon the fire is out.

The grace notes are for the piano and should not be sung.

The Busy Postman

MABEL E. BRAY

OLD ENGLISH MELODY

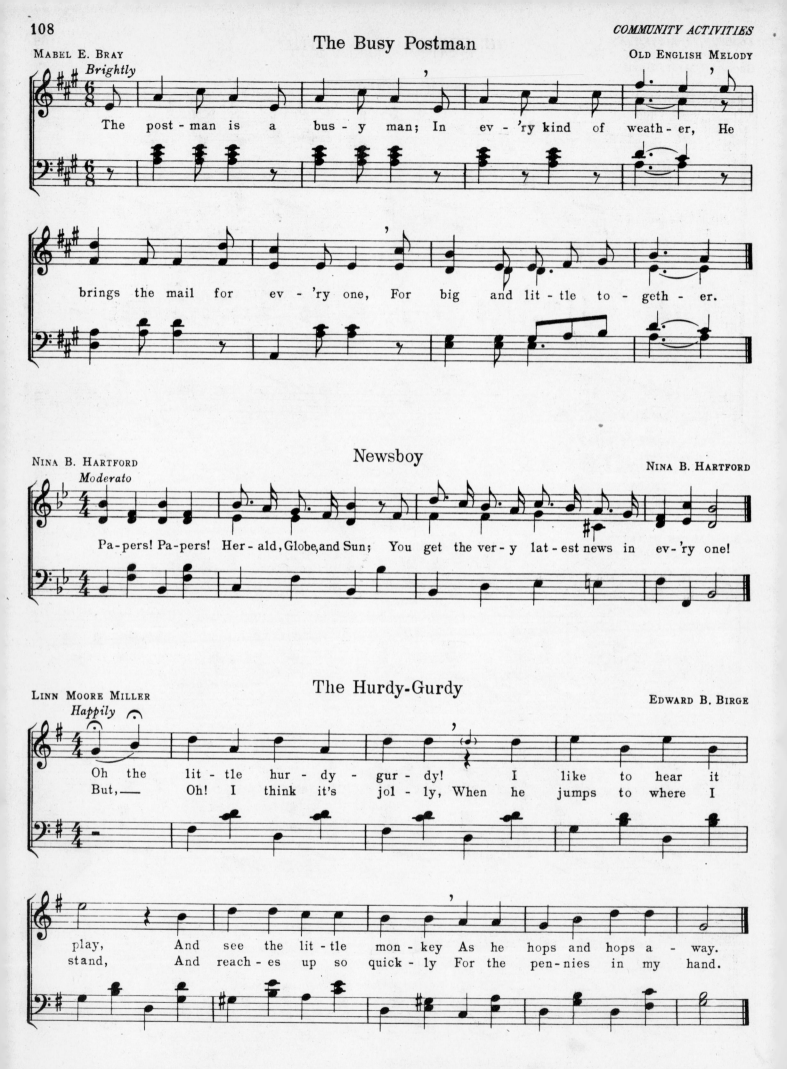

The post-man is a bus-y man; In ev-'ry kind of weath-er, He

brings the mail for ev-'ry one, For big and lit-tle to-geth-er.

Newsboy

NINA B. HARTFORD

NINA B. HARTFORD

Pa-pers! Pa-pers! Her-ald, Globe, and Sun; You get the ver-y lat-est news in ev-'ry one!

The Hurdy-Gurdy

LINN MOORE MILLER

EDWARD B. BIRGE

Oh the lit-tle hur-dy-gur-dy! I like to hear it
But,— Oh! I think it's jol-ly, When he jumps to where I

play, And see the lit-tle mon-key As he hops and hops a-way.
stand, And reach-es up so quick-ly For the pen-nies in my hand.

The Street-Cleaner Man

GEORGE S. APPLEGARTH

W. OTTO MIESSNER

In waltz tempo

Sweep,—— Sweep,—— Sweep goes the street-clean-er man,—— Dressed all in white with his broom and his can;—— Scrape,—— Scrape,—— Scrape as he brush-es the street;—— Teach - ing us all to be tid - y and neat.——

On the Way to School

BLANCHE JENNINGS THOMPSON

L. LESLIE LOTH

In marching tempo

What a lot of things to see, On the way to school!—— Squir-rels run-ning
What a lot of things to hear, On the way to school!—— Some one whis-tles

up a tree, On the way to school.—— Spar-rows build-ing cun-ning nests,
loud and clear, On the way to school.—— Work-men's ham-mers go, bing, bang!

Rob - ins smooth-ing down their vests, What a lot of things to see, On the way to school!
Fire chief's gong goes, clang, clang, clang! What a lot of things to hear, On the way to school!

The Trolley Man

MAY MORGAN

GEORGE LeROY LINDSAY

Happily

The trol-ley-man when he goes by 'Most al-ways waves to

ding dong me,___ I'm sure he knows when I am grown A trol-ley-man I'll be.___

The Farmer

MABEL E. BRAY

OLD NURSERY SONG

Brightly

I sell but-ter, I sell cheese, I sell hon-ey made by bees;

I sell corn and I sell wheat, Big red ap-ples, round and sweet.

The Old Woman

CHINESE MOTHER GOOSE RHYME

EDWARD B. BIRGE

Moderato

There was an old wom-an, As I have heard tell, She
She hur-ried back home, But her door-step was high, She

went to sell pie, But her pie would not sell.
stum-bled and fell, And a dog ate her pie.

Bread and Cherries

WALTER DE LA MARE

JAMES H. ROGERS

Not too fast, and well accented

, a little more softly

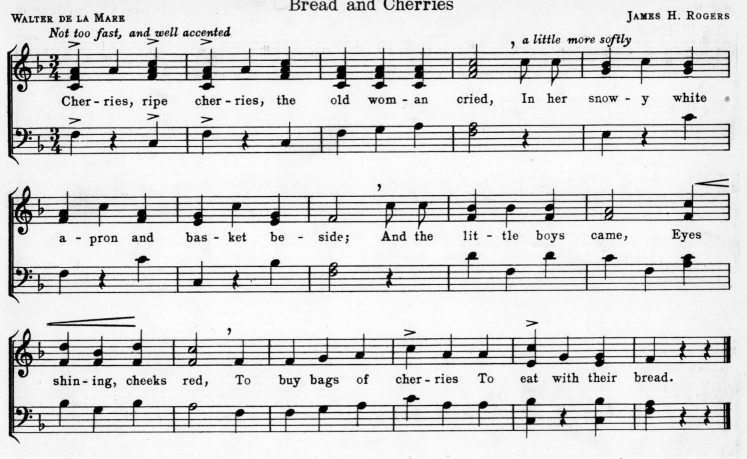

Cher-ries, ripe cher-ries, the old wom-an cried, In her snow-y white a-pron and bas-ket be-side; And the lit-tle boys came, Eyes shin-ing, cheeks red, To buy bags of cher-ries To eat with their bread.

The Delicatessen Store

ELEANOR ALLETTA CHAFFEE

DANIEL PROTHEROE

Moderato

The— del-i-ca-tes-sen has so man-y things, That I scarce-ly— know what I shall buy;— There are sal-ads and chees-es and pret-zels in rings, And— fish-cakes all read-y to fry.—

There are cans— full of ev-'ry-thing un-der the sun, And— jel-lies and pick-les and meat;— I— don't know where else it would be so much fun To se-lect what I'm go-ing to eat.—

The Candy Shop

LINN MOORE MILLER

LINN MOORE MILLER

Brightly

Come and buy a lol - ly - pop, At the lit - tle can - dy shop,

Chil - dren have your pen - nies hand - y, Step this way and buy some can - dy.

The Five and Ten Cent Store

ELEANOR ALLETTA CHAFFEE

NURSERY TUNE

Not too quickly

What shall I buy for a nick-el or dime? A lit - tle toy watch to tell me the time, A
What shall I buy with my mon-ey to-day? A book and some cray-ons with col-ors so gay, A

train that will run on a ti - ny tin track, Or a doz - en bright mar-bles sewed up in a sack?
pad and a pen-cil to write or to draw, A puz-zle, a top, or a ham-mer and saw?

The Baker's Shop

ELEANOR ALLETTA CHAFFEE

FRANCIS FINDLAY

Allegretto

The bak - er's shop is spick and span, The bread is fresh from shin - y pan; The
The rolls are brown as brown can be, And all the pies are fair to see; The

cakes are dressed in pa - per lace, And each is in its prop - er place.
cook - ies seem to say, "Oh, my! How you will like us by and by!"

The Busy Cobbler

George S. Applegarth

Harriet Ware

In waltz tempo

Tip-pi-ty, tip-pi-ty, tap, tap, tap, The cob-bler pounds on his big, stout lap; He

tick - tacks one and he tick - tacks two, And he makes old shoes al-most like new.

cresc. ... *rit.*

Tip-pi - ty, tip-pi -ty tap, tap, tap, The cob - bler pounds on his big, stout lap.

The Carpenters' Song

Nina B. Hartford

Nina B. Hartford

Happily

1. To - day we are car - pen - ters one and all, See how we saw, see
2. We climb up the lad - ders to reach the roof, Up, up we climb, up,
3. We pound and we ham - mer the whole day long, See how we pound, see

how we saw; We're build-ing a house that is straight and tall, That's why we saw to-
up we climb; Our build-ing, you know, must be weath - er proof, That's why we climb to-
how we pound; What - ev - er we build must be tight and strong, That's why we pound to-

day.___ We march a - round our house and sing, While more wood and nails we bring.
day.___ We march a - round our house and sing, While more wood and nails we bring.
day.___ Now skip and sing, our house is done; Play - ing car-pen-ter's heaps of fun.

The Barber

Linn Moore Miller

Paul Ambrose

Allegretto

I love to sit in the bar-ber's chair, And feel the snip, snip, snip, on my hair; I
like the brush all__ nice and clean; And oh! the smell of the bril - lian-tine!

The Town Clock

Translation by Mabel E. Bray

French Nursery Song

Rather slowly

Far up in the stee - ple tower, Bells are ring - ing ev - 'ry hour, Sing-ing
Hear the ring - ing sweet and clear! To the peo - ple far and near,

day and night this song: Ding, ding, dong; Ding, ding, dong; Ding, ding, dong; Ding, ding, dong.

If I'd as Much Money

Mother Goose

William A. White

Allegretto

If I'd as much mon-ey as I could spend, I nev-er would cry, "Old chairs to mend, Old
If I'd as much mon-ey as I could tell, I nev-er would cry, "Old clothes to sell, Old

chairs to mend, old chairs to mend;" I nev - er would cry, "Old chairs to mend."
clothes to sell, old clothes to sell;" I nev - er would cry, "Old clothes to sell."

Concerning Travel

Caroline Hofman*

G. A. Grant-Schaefer

Allegretto

The light-ning ex-press goes rush-ing through With a scream, a toot, and a
The light-ning ex-press is fun to see, But I like the lo-cal, it

rit.

great to-do; But the slow old lo-cal just moves a-long Like an old-time song.
stops for me; I like the lo-cal, it stops for me, It stops for me.

From St. Nicholas, by permission of the Century Co.

Engines

Mabel E. Bray

French Nursery Song

Moderato

Chug, chug, chug! The en-gine's go-ing; Ding, ding, dong! The bell rings
En-gines bring us food and cloth-ing, Bring us books and sweets and

too; Toot, toot, toot! The en-gine whis-tles, "Clear the track!" for me and you.
toys; Ev-'ry-bod-y likes the en-gines; Most of all the girls and boys!

On the Bus

George S. Applegarth

Daniel Protheroe

Allegretto

I love to ride on the roll-ing bus, High up in a seat on top, As
But if I ev-er could have my way, It nev-er would stop at all, But

cresc.

light and eas-y it car-ries us Wher-ev-er we wish to stop.
roll a-way all the sum-mer day, 'Till time for my sup-per call.

cresc.

The Motor Car

Linn Moore Miller

Linn Moore Miller

Honk! honk! honk! In my mo-tor car we go; Honk! honk!

honk! Ver-y fast and ver-y slow; It seems to me the things we pass, Go

by us, oh! so ver-y fast! Honk! honk! honk! Honk! honk!

The Aeroplane

George S. Applegarth

W. Otto Miessner

Zoom! goes the aer-o-plane up in the sky,____

Hums like a bum-ble-bee buz-zing on high,____ Looks ver-y much like a big drag-on

fly;____ Now it is gone, Mis-ter Fly-er, "Good - by!"

Rain

MARGARET A. FASSITT

GEORGE LEROY LINDSAY

For-ty lit-tle rain-drops On the win-dow-pane,

For-ty lit-tle rain-drops Danc-ing there a-gain. Hear them pit-ter-pat-ter,

Is-n't it great fun? But for-ty lit-tle rain-drops Chase a-way the sun!

The Brook

MARGARET A. FASSITT

EDWARD A. MUELLER

Lit-tle brook, pret-ty brook, Sing-ing as you go;

Rip-pling o'er the mead-ow, Neith-er fast nor slow.

The River

EDITH LANHAM BOKELOH

FRANCIS FINDLAY

In the time of a slow waltz

1. The riv-er runs a-long,_____ I like its gen-tle
2. The riv-er runs a-way,_____ I watch it ev-'ry
3. It goes right by the town,_____ And un-der bridg-es

song;_____ It flows so swift-ly by,_____ As blue
day;_____ It pass-es by the trees,_____ It
brown;_____ Where does the riv-er go?_____ Does

1st time

_____ as the blue_____ sky.

2nd and 3rd times

poco rall.

rip-ples in the breeze._____
an-y-bod-y know?_____

The Sea

Reprinted by permission from "For Days and Days," A Year-round Treasury of Verse for Children, by Annette Wynne. Copyright, 1919, by Frederick A. Stokes Company

ANNETTE WYNNE

DANIEL PROTHEROE

Moderato misterioso

The sea comes roll-ing up the land, And plays a game a-long the sand; But

cresc.

when the chil-dren want to play, The sea just laughs and runs a-way.

Ships

MAY MORGAN

ANICE TERHUNE

Smoothly and swingingly

Down the bay the ships go sail - ing, Sail - ing off to sea,___

Sail - ing off to dis - tant coun - tries, Where I'd like to be.___

A Sea Song from the Shore

JAMES WHITCOMB RILEY

MARSHALL BARTHOLOMEW

With spirit

rugged, well accented

Hail! ho! Sail! ho! A-hoy! A-hoy! A-hoy! Who calls me so far at sea? On-ly a lit-tle boy!

Sail! ho! Hail! ho! The sail - or loves the sea; I wish that he would cap - ture,

Wish that he would cap - ture A lit - tle sea - horse and send him back to me.

SAILOR DANCE

Well accented throughout

The Wind

TRADITIONAL

OLD ENGLISH

1. When the wind is in the East, It's nei - ther good for
2. When the wind is in the West, The corn and clo - ver
3. When the jol - ly North - wind blows, It brings the cold and
4. When the gen - tle South - wind blows, The flow'rs their pet - als

man nor beast, It's nei - ther good for man nor beast.
grow the best, The corn and clo - ver grow the best.
drift - ing snows, It brings the cold and drift - ing snows.
all un - close, The flow'rs their pet - als all un - close.

My Kite

MAUDE M. GRANT

DANIEL PROTHEROE

Allegretto cantabile

Up in the sky, so ver - y high, I let my pret - ty new kite fly, Like a

bird on the wing, But I hold the string, And it will come back to me by and by.

From "Choice Pieces for Primary Pupils," by permission of F.A.Owen Publishing Company.

Clouds

HELEN de LORENZI

EDWARD A. MUELLER

Simply

The gay lit - tle white clouds go sail - ing by, Light fluf - fy white pil - lows in the sky.

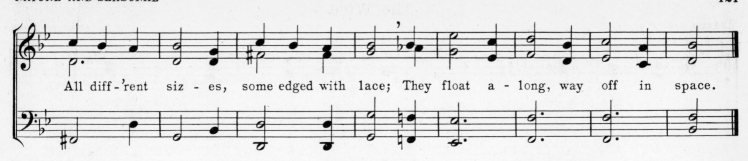

All diff-'rent siz - es, some edged with lace; They float a - long, way off in space.

The Man-in-the-Moon

IRMENGARD CHARLTON HORN

IRMENGARD CHARLTON HORN

Simply

Have you ev - er seen the Man - in - the - Moon? If you watch you may see him ver - y

soon; He'll come sail-ing through the sky, Where he lives way up on high. "Oh, Man-in-the-Moon, come soon!"

When the Stars

From ST. NICHOLAS
By permission of the Century Co.

DR. GARRETT

Moderato

When the stars at set of sun Twin - kle in the sky,___ Then the lit - tle
Then, when morn-ing light ap-pears And the bright sun gleams,___ Babes and birds and

pp slowly

babes at rest Dream that moth - er's by,___ Dream that moth - er's by.___
flow - ers, too, Wake from sweet - est dreams, Wake from sweet - est dreams.

Summer and Winter

Rebecca B. Foresman

Nursery Song

Moderato

I do not know which I love best, Be - cause, when sum - mer's
And when some morn - ing I a - wake, The ground is white with

here, I wish that sum - mer time would last Much long - er than a year.
snow; And then I wish the win - ter days Would nev - er, nev - er go.

Leaves in Autumn

Carolyn Hall Grant

Anice Terhune

Rather Quickly

Red leaves and bronze leaves, Cin-na-mon and gold; See, I've fill'd my bas-ket As full as it will hold.

Autumn Fires

Agnes Choate Wonson

Edward B. Birge

Moderato

Green leaves turn to red and yel - low, Jack Frost paints them all;———

Then they change to or - ange sparks In bon - fires in the fall.———

The Leaves are Gone

NINA B. HARTFORD

NINA B. HARTFORD

The leaves are gone from the ma-ple trees The branch-es all are bare; The
The riv-er soon will hush its song In i-cy blank-ets deep; The

birds have left their lit-tle nests; Jack Frost is ev-'ry-where.
fields and flow'rs be-neath the snow 'Til spring will lie a-sleep.

I'd Like to be a Farmer

CAROLYN E. SLOAT

L. LESLIE LOTH

Moderato

I'd like to be a farm-er And plant my field with seeds; I'd wa-ter them and

care for them, And keep them free from weeds. And when the corn and yel-low squash Had

ri-pened in the fall, I'd take them to the mar-ket place And there I'd sell them all.

Autumn and Winter Winds

MABEL E. BRAY

FRENCH FOLK SONG

(All) *(One group)* *(Another group)* *(All)*

The wind is moan-ing Oo, oo, oo,——— oo, Oo, oo,——— oo, Au-tumn days are near.
The wind is howl-ing Oo, oo, oo,——— oo, Oo, oo,——— oo, Win-ter days are near.

The North Wind Doth Blow

MOTHER GOOSE

J. W. ELLIOTT

Sadly

The North Wind doth blow, And we shall have snow, And what will poor Rob-in do then.— He'll

sit in the barn, And keep him-self warm, And tuck his head un-der his wing, Poor thing!

Snowflakes

MARY MAPES DODGE

DANIEL PROTHEROE

Allegretto

(Child)

(Snowflakes)

Lit-tle white feath-ers fill-ing the air, Lit-tle white feath-ers, How came you there? We

came from the cloud-birds Fly-ing so high, Shak-ing their white wings Up in the sky.

Skating

W. Otto Miessner

W. Otto Miessner

Heartily

The ice is froz-en smooth and sound, And all the boys a-round____ Are there with sing-ing, shout-ing mates, To fly on sil-ver skates.____ They swerve and curve, They slide and glide, And form in col-umns wide.____

The Snowman

Linn Moore Miller

Linn Moore Miller

Moderately quick

There's a lit-tle old man made of snow,____ He stands on guard all the day;____ ____ Like a sol-dier bold he fears not the cold; But the sun makes him run a-way!____

Snowflake Feathers

MABEL E. BRAY

L. LESLIE LOTH

Soft - ly, soft - ly, fall - ing down, Sprink - ling feath - ers on the town;

Pret - ty snow - flakes, ver - y white,— Blow, and glis - ten in the light.

The Dressed-Up Town

ELLA D. WATKINS

PAUL AMBROSE

You ought to see our pret - ty town, You'd hard - ly know the

place; It's dress'd up in a snow - y gown All trim'd with i - cy lace!

Dance ad lib.

January and February

CHRISTINA ROSSETTI
Moderato

MODERN MUSIC SERIES

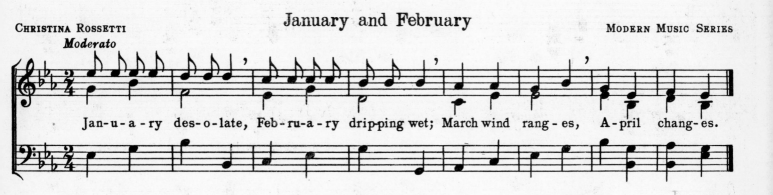

Jan-u-a-ry des-o-late, Feb-ru-a-ry drip-ping wet; March wind rang-es, A-pril chang-es.

March

LOUISE AYRES GARNETT
Andantino

G. A. GRANT-SCHAEFER

I know where March is, O-ver the hill; In a brown a-pron Cud-dled and still.
Earth has her pock-ets Brim-ming with Spring, Emp-ties them out When dick-y birds sing.

The Willow Cats

MARGARET WIDDEMER
Allegretto

FRENCH NURSERY SONG

They call them Pus-sy Wil-lows, But there's not a cat to
see,— Ex-cept the lit-tle fur-ry toes That stick out on the tree.—

Spring

Christina Rossetti   Harriet Ware

Such a bright day, With the sun glow-ing, And the trees half in leaf And the grass grow-ing;

Such a bright day, With the sun glow-ing, And the trees half in leaf And the grass grow-ing.

Spring Flowers

Margaret A. Fassitt   Harriet Ware

See the mer-ry daf-fo-dils, Nod-ding gai-ly from the hills;

Vio-lets blue and may-flow'rs fair, Spring up al-most an-y-where.

Rain in April

Eleanor Hammond

Paul Ambrose

Allegretto

Rain has such fun in A-pril, It pat-ters through the trees,__

Talk-ing to all the leaf buds And rob-ins that it sees.__

Jack-in-the-Pulpit

Clara Smith

James H. Rogers

Rather loudly and sturdily

Jack-in-the-pul-pit preach-es to-day, Un-der the green trees, Just

Not so loudly

o-ver the way, Un-der the green trees, Just o-ver the way.

Early Spring

Margaret A. Fassitt

G. A. Grant-Schaefer

Allegretto
mp

I'm a lit-tle frog, Just a Pol-ly-wog; I live in the brook un-der-neath the log.

And be-cause it's spring, Spring, spring, spring, I'm so hap-py that I have to Sing, sing, sing!

Lady Daffadown

CHRISTINA ROSSETTI

MODERN MUSIC SERIES

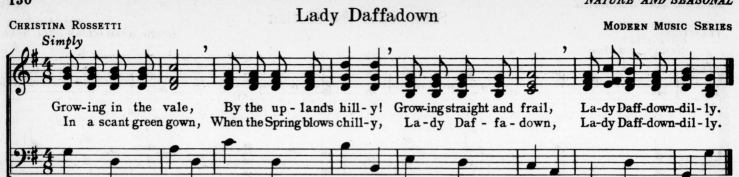

Grow-ing in the vale, By the up-lands hill-y! Grow-ing straight and frail, La-dy Daff-down-dil-ly.
In a scant green gown, When the Spring blows chill-y, La-dy Daf-fa-down, La-dy Daff-down-dil-ly.

Rain in Summer

ALDIS DUNBAR

L. LESLIE LOTH

The sum-mer sun was shin-ing, shin-ing, Out of a clear blue sky; The
The love-ly clouds came sail-ing, sail-ing, Bring-ing a rain-y day; And

lit-tle brooks ran soft-ly, soft-ly, Half of their peb-bles dry.
all the brooks ran splash-ing, splash-ing, Laugh-ing a-long their way.

The Bee

LINN MOORE MILLER

LINN MOORE MILLER

In-to the blos-som goes the bee To gath-er sweets for his fam-i-ly; He

helps him-self, as he al-ways does, Then off he flies home a-gain, buzz, buzz, buzz!

Sing, Said the Mother

TRADITIONAL

SOUTH APPALACHIAN FOLK SONG

Simply, not slow

Over in the mead-ows in the nest in the tree, Lived an old moth-er bird-y and her lit-tle bird-ies three. "Sing," said the moth-er; "We sing," said the three, So they sang and were glad in the nest in the tree.

Butterfly and Honeybee

LINN MOORE MILLER

LINN MOORE MILLER

Allegretto

One day in my gar-den, oh, what did I see! A but-ter-fly chas-ing a hon-ey-bee! They tagged and they danced, And when that was through, They played hide and seek in the vi-o-lets blue.

The Gardener

George E. Thompson Jr.

Harriet Ware

Simply

Out in the gar - den, wa-ter-ing flow'rs, The gar - d'ner will stay for hours, He

mows the grass and plants the seeds, And works all day to pull the weeds!

Swinging

Blanche Jennings Thompson

Edward A. Mueller

Slow waltz

Swing - ing, swing - ing, Out in the or - chard swing.

Swing - ing, swing - ing, This is the song we sing.

The Robin

Lawrence Alma Tadema

Edward B. Birge

Simply

When fa - ther takes his spade to dig, Then rob - in comes a -

long; He sits up - on a lit - tle twig, And sings a lit - tle song.

Pansies

Katharine Lee Bates

W. Otto Miessner

Allegretto

Pan - sies wear!__ Pan - sies wear!__ Pur - ples wov - en
Pan - sies wear!__ Look at me!__ Gleam - y yel - lows,

Out of air,_____ Out of air; Dew and sun, Pur - ple pan - sies,
Good to see!_____ Good to see! In the sun, Mer - ry fel - lows;

1.
I_____ am__ one!_____

2.
I_____ am__ one!_____

Oak Trees

Mrs. Arthur L. Moore

Edward A. Mueller

Broad

Oh, green old trees, how old are you? How man - y, man - y years Since you were

new? 'Tis strange that ba - by a - corns small Could grow to oaks so big and tall!

Baby Birds

MABEL E. BRAY

FRENCH NURSERY SONG

Sleep, sleep, ba-by birds. Soft-ly swings your cra-dle high; Rock, rock in your nest, Breez-es sing your lul-la-by.

Feeding the Birds

KATHARINE LEE BATES

EDWARD A. MUELLER

From fall to spring, 'Tis a lit-tle thing To_ spread the birds good cheer. On a win-dow tray, Where the birds may play At sum-mer all the year.

The Secret

Attributed to
THOMAS GAINSBOROUGH

HORATIO PARKER

We have a se-cret, just we three, The rob-in and I and the sweet cher-ry tree. The bird told the tree and the tree told me, And no-bod-y knows it but just we three.

The Bobolink

HELEN LOUISE CLARK

W. OTTO MIESSNER

I real-ly think the bo-bo-link Is feath-er'd up-side down! He

wears his black up - on his breast, And white up - on his crown!

Birds

AGNES CHOATE WONSON

DANIEL PROTHEROE

The blue - bird has a coat of blue, The rob - in wears a vest of

red; The chick - a - dee is speck-led brown, The crow is black from tail to head.

Lily Bells

VIRGINIA BAKER

HORATIO PARKER

Lil - y bells ring, Gay rob-ins sing, Chil - dren are hap-py For now it is spring.

The Owl

NINA B. HARTFORD

NINA B. HARTFORD

On a sum-mer night when the moon is bright, Mis-ter Owl screams, "Whoo! Whoo!

Whoo!"____ Lit-tle Mice, run and hide, for his eyes, big and wide, Are

look-ing for you, you, you!____ Yes they're look-ing for you, you, you!

The Mocking Bird

MAY MORGAN

W. OTTO MIESSNER

Of all the sing-ing birds I know, The mock-ing bird sings the best;

He has one song that's ver-y long

The Oriole's Nest

MAY MORGAN   HARRIET WARE

Allegretto

The o-ri-ole's nest is a bas - ket, A bas - ket, a bas - ket; The o-ri-ole's nest is a

bas - ket, Swing-ing from a bough.— And there in the bas-ket a - sway - ing, a-

sway - ing, a - sway - ing, And there in the bas-ket a - sway - ing, Are five wee ba - bies now!—

My Dog

Agnes Choate Wonson

Francis Findlay

I have a dog all shag-gy, His ears are rough and rag-gy, And with his tongue, so soft and pink, He kiss-es me, quick as a wink!

Kitty White

Mother Goose

Paul Ambrose

Kit-ty White so sly-ly comes To catch the Mous-ie Gray;

Mous-ie hears her soft-ly creep, And quick-ly runs a-way.

A Rabbit

ELIZABETH MADOX ROBERTS

LINN MOORE MILLER

Allegretto

A rab-bit works its ears and tries To see you with its rab-bit eyes. Its

sau-cy lit-tle tail it flounc-es, And when it hits the ground it bounc-es.

The Waggley Dog

ALDIS DUNBAR

DANIEL PROTHEROE

Brightly

My pup-py's coat is black and brown, His tongue is pink and shin-y. I
It's like a lit-tle curl-y bunch Up-on my darl-ing Ro-ver. So

brush his hair, I smooth him down; But oh, his tail is ti-ny.
when I call him in to lunch, He has to wag all o-ver.

Gray Squirrel

VIRGINIA BAKER

G. A. GRANT-SCHAEFER

Moderato

Down from the trees the nuts are fall-ing, While lit-tle squir-rels gray

Hide them a-way in hol-low tree trunks, Work-ing the live-long day.

Gray Squirrels

ANNIE M. CLARKE OSTRANDER

ANNIE M. CLARKE OSTRANDER

Little Bunny Rabbit

ANNIE M. CLARKE OSTRANDER

ANNIE M. CLARKE OSTRANDER

Caterpillar

AGNES CHOATE WONSON

EDWARD A. MUELLER

Allegro

Oh, cat-er-pil-lar fur-ry, You seem in such a hur-ry; Un-der-neath some leaf or stone, Do you live there all a-lone?

The Friendly Cow

ROBERT LOUIS STEVENSON

EDWARD B. BIRGE

Simply

The friend-ly cow, all red and white, I love with all my heart;— She gives me cream with all her might, To eat with ap-ple tart.—

Who Likes the Rain?

CLARA DOTY BATES

G. A. GRANT-SCHAEFER

In march time

"I," said the duck, "I call it fun, For I have my lit-tle red rub-bers on; They make a cun-ning three-toed track In the soft, cool mud! Quack! Quack! Quack!"

Baa, Baa, Black Sheep

J. W. ELLIOTT

Baa, baa, black sheep, Have you an-y wool? Yes sir, yes sir, Three bags full;
One for my mas-ter, One for my dame, But none for the lit-tle boy Who cries in the lane.

Frogs at School

GEORGE COOPER

EDWARD B. BIRGE

Twen-ty frog-gies went to school, Down be-side a rush-y pool;
Twen-ty lit-tle coats of green, Twen-ty vests all white and clean.

Shear the Sheep

TRADITIONAL

J. W. ELLIOTT

Shear the sheep and trim the tree, But let the lit-tle lamb go free.

My Hen

Edith Lanham Bokeloh

Daniel Protheroe

Allegretto

I love to watch my speck - led hen, With all her chicks a - bout her; And
see them scam - per when she clucks, What would I do with - out her!

In Fairyland

Julia W. Bingham

James H. Rogers

Lively

1. The Light - ning Bug, the Light - ning Bug, I won - der if you
2. The Bum - ble Bee, the Bum - ble Bee, How swift - ly he can
3. The But - ter - fly, the But - ter - fly, It's real - ly tru - ly

know How much the fair - ies love him? He is their ra - di -
sail. He is the fair - ies' post - man, And car - ries all the
so, He is the fair - ies' air - plane; They ride him to and

o._____ The Light - ning Bug, the Light - ning Bug, The fair - ies' ra - di - o.
mail._____ The Bum - ble Bee, the Bum - ble Bee; He car - ries fair - y mail.
fro._____ The But - ter - fly, the But - ter - fly; They ride him to and fro.

The Zoo

LINN MOORE MILLER

G. A. GRANT-SCHAEFER

Moderato

Of all the wild an-i-mals in the zoo, The
O, I'm ver-y fond of the po-lar bear, And

queer-est I think is the kan-ga-roo; The fierce old li-ons and
all of the an-i-mals ev-'ry-where; I won-der what they would

ti-gers, too, Just stare and swish their tails at you.
be a-bout, If cag-es were o-pened and they got out.

Five Little White Mice

MRS. F. A. B. DUNNING

GERMAN POPULAR AIR

Allegretto

Five lit-tle white mice Found a box full of rice; And they

went to the top, With a squeal and a hop, To eat all the rice They were

sure was so nice; Five lit-tle white mice In a box full of rice!

At the Circus

MAY MORGAN

ANICE TERHUNE

Cir - cus folk have lots of fun, Wear - ing pret - ty span - gled things;

Rid - ing pranc - ing hors - es, too, Round and round and round the rings!

The Dove

W. OTTO MIESSNER

W. OTTO MIESSNER

Fly, pret - ty dove, Far o'er the sea; Car - ry my

love To Dol - ly Ma - rie.____ Then hur - ry home, Fly, quick - ly;

Oh! Tell me my Dol - ly's well, Moth - er must know!____

V. MOTHER GOOSE

Humpty Dumpty

MOTHER GOOSE

J. W. ELLIOTT

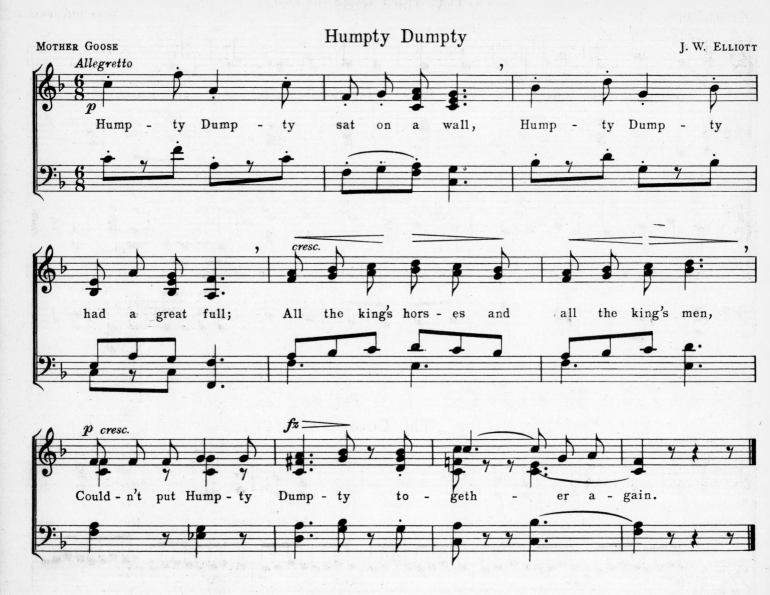

Humpty Dumpty sat on a wall, Humpty Dumpty had a great full; All the king's horses and all the king's men, Couldn't put Humpty Dumpty together again.

Mary, Mary, Quite Contrary

MOTHER GOOSE

W. A. WHITE

Mary, Mary, quite contrary; How does your garden grow? "With silver bells and cockle shells, And pretty maids all in a row."

Hark, Hark, the Dogs do Bark

MOTHER GOOSE

HORATIO PARKER

Allegro resoluto

Hark, hark, the dogs do bark, The beg-gars have come to town.

Some in rags and some in tags And some in vel-vet gowns.

The King of France

MOTHER GOOSE

J. W. ELLIOTT

Allegretto moderato
With decision

The King of France with four thou-sand men Draw their swords, and put them up a-gain.

Old King Cole

MOTHER GOOSE

OLD ENGLISH

Allegretto

Old King Cole was a mer-ry old soul, And a mer-ry old soul was he. He

called for his pipe And he called for his bowl And he called for his fid-dlers three. Twee-dee, twee-dee,

twee-dee, twee-dee, went his fid-dlers three; Twee-dee, twee-dee, twee-dee, twee-dee, went his fid-dlers three!

Columbus

MABEL E. BRAY

SPANISH MELODY

Brightly

O sing to Co - lum - bus, Who sailed o'er the sea,___ To find this bon - ny land of ours, The land for you and me!___

Hallowe'en

Words and Music by
Class in Public School Music,
New Jersey Teachers' College

Mysteriously

To - night we'll see some big black cats; And witch - es we will meet;___ While boys and girls in fun - ny clothes Will run a - bout the street.___

Salute the Flag

MABEL E. BRAY

OLD ARMY CALL

In marching tempo

Hold it up high, Close to the sky; Red, White and Blue, to you we are true.

Hats in your hand, Straight you must stand; Al - ways sa - lute the Red, White and Blue.

Thanksgiving Day

EDNA COBB DUTCHER

W. OTTO MIESSNER

Moderato

The pump-kin has not a word to say, The tur-key is feel - ing sad.____ To-mor-row will be Thanks-giv-ing day; And how could they feel glad? And how could they feel glad?

Merry Christmas

NINA B. HARTFORD

NINA B. HARTFORD

Brightly

Mer - ry Christ-mas, Mer - ry Christ-mas, On this bright and hap - py day.

Mer - ry Christ-mas, Mer - ry Christ-mas, All our stock-ings seem to say;

San - ta Claus did not for - get us, Such a lot of toys he left us,

Mer - ry Christ-mas, Mer - ry Christ-mas, O'er the whole wide world to - day!

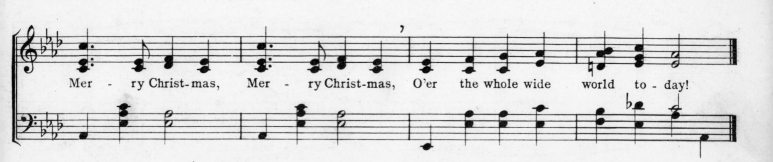

Christmas Bells

Edith L Bokeloh

Paul Bliss

Ring the mer - ry, mer - ry bells, Their hap - py song of Christ - mas tells; Of

San - ta Claus and Christ - mas joys, And stock - ings brim - ming full of toys.

The New Year

Anonymous

Daniel Protheroe

O, I am the lit - tle New Year, ho! ho! Here I come trip-ping it o - ver the snow;

Shak - ing my bells with a mer - ry din, So o - pen the doors and let me in.

Lincoln

Edna Cobb Dutcher

W. Otto Miessner

Moderato

We love the name of Lin-coln, For him a song we sing; His
birth to-day we cel-e-brate, And grate-ful prais-es bring.

Washington and the Flag

Mabel E. Bray

W. Otto Miessner

Moderato

George Wash-ing-ton, George Wash-ing-ton, We sing to-day of you; You
George Wash-ing-ton, George Wash-ing-ton, We sing to-day of you, And

fought to make our coun-try free; You were our lead-er true.
wave on high our star-ry flag; Our own red, white and blue.

Valentines

Anna L. Whitmore

Franz Schubert

Allegretto

Val-en-tines so bright and gay, We are send-ing out to-day,

With a mes-sage, "I love you; Tell me that you love me too!"

Making a Valentine

W. Otto Miessner
Brightly

W. Otto Miessner

Val - en - tine! Val - en - tine! Pic - tures bright and lac - es fine.

Val - en - tine! Val - en - tine! When it's made, I'll give you mine.

Easter Eggs

Virginia Baker
Brightly

Edward B. Birge

1. Eas - ter eggs! Eas - ter eggs! What a pret - ty sight;
2. Eas - ter eggs! Eas - ter eggs! Tied with rib - bons gay;
3. Eas - ter eggs! Eas - ter eggs! Dain - ty gifts I think;

Blue and gold and sil - ver, Lav - en - der and white.
Brown and green and scar - let, Yel - low, mauve, and gray.
Crim - son, lem - on, or - ange, Ol - ive, se - pia, pink.

An Arbor Day Tree

Author unknown
Gently and wistfully

Anice Terhune

Dear lit - tle tree that we plant to - day,___ What will you be when we're old and gray?

May Basket

LINN MOORE MILLER   LINN MOORE MILLER

Cheerful

A tis - ket, a tas - ket, a wee dain - ty bas - ket; All filled up with

bon - bons and flow - ers so gay.___ A tis - ket, a tas - ket, a

pret - ty May bas - ket; All wait - ing for you on this hap - py May day.___

Flag Day

ANNA L. WHITMORE   BUGLE CALL, "ASSEMBLY"

Brightly

Sing a song a - bout our flag, See the col - ors wav - ing high.

All sa - lute, all sa - lute, When the flag pass - es by.

America

SAMUEL F. SMITH   HENRY CAREY

Moderato

My coun - try! 'tis of thee, Sweet land of lib - er - ty, Of thee I sing; Land where my

fa - thers died, Land of the Pil - grims' pride, From ev - 'ry___ moun - tain side, Let free - dom ring.

The Big Drum

MALCOLM DOUGLAS
From "St. Nicholas" by permission of The Century Company

MARK SEELY

A lit-tle man bought him a big bass drum, Boom, boom, boom!___ "Who

knows," said he, "When a war will come?" Boom, boom, boom!___ "I'm

not at all fright-ened, you un-der-stand; But if I am called on to fight for my land, I

want to be read-y to play in the band;" Boom, boom, boom!___

Yankee Doodle

OLD SONG

Vivace

Yank-ee Doo-dle went to town, Up-on a lit-tle po-ny; He stuck a feath-er

in his cap And called it Ma-ca-ro-ni. Tra-la-la-la-la-la-la;

Tra-la-la-la-la-la, Tra-la-la-la-la-la-la, He called it Ma-ca-ro-ni!

Fiddles and Horns

MABEL E. BRAY

OLD FRENCH TUNE

Brightly

"Mm;"_____ The fid-dles sing; "Toot, toot-toot-toot-toot-toot," the

big horns ring! The fid-dles sing-ing, The horns a-ring-ing, "Mm;"_____

(Fiddles)

"Toot-toot, toot, toot" Mm_____ Mm_____

(Horns) Toot-toot-toot-toot-toot-toot-toot-toot-toot-toot-toot-toot-toot-

Mm_____   Mm_____

toot-toot-toot-toot-toot-toot-toot-toot-toot-toot-toot-toot-toot-toot-toot-toot-toot.

Swing Song

Agnes Choate Wonson

W. Otto Miessner

Andantino

Swing high, Swing low, Swing fast, Swing slow;

I like to swing____ Best of an - y - thing! ____

The Child and the Sparrow

Thomas Westwood

G. A. Grant-Schaefer

With a swinging motion

mf (Child)

(Sparrow)

Spar-row in the cher-ry tree, cher-ry tree, Won't you drop one down for me? Pre - sent-ly.
Sau - cy Spar-row, cease your fun, cease your fun, What! you're off, and gave me none! All are gone!

Nineteen Birds

Mother Goose

J. W. Elliott

Moderato

1. Nine - teen birds and one bird more, Just make twen - ty and that's a score.
2. To the score then add but one; That will make just twen - ty one.
3. Now add two, and you will see, You have made up twen - ty three.
4. If you like these clev - er tricks, Add three more for twen - ty six.
5. Then three more, if you have time; Now you've got to twen - ty nine.
6. Twen - ty - nine now quick - ly take, Add one more and thir - ty make.

Playing Indian

Blanche Jennings Thompson

George LeRoy Lindsay

In Indian style

Hoo, hoo, hoo! Hoo, hoo, hoo! I'm an In-dian chief to-
Hoo, hoo, hoo! Hoo, hoo, hoo! I'm an In-dian squaw to-

day. I have a gun and tom-a-hawk, And a feath-er head-dress gay!
day. I have a lit-tle brown pa-poose, And a strings of beads so gay!

Sing Me a Song

Christina Rossetti

James H. Rogers

In moderate time but without dragging *a little faster*

Sing me a song. What shall I sing? Three mer-ry sis-ters,

more slowly *quite softly*

Danc-ing in a ring. Sing, sing, Sing me a song.

My Scooter

Blanche Jennings Thompson

G. A. Grant-Schaefer

Allegretto
mf

I have a new red scoot-er; You'd bet-ter clear the

track. I scoot down to the cor-ner, And then come scoot-ing back.

Looby Loo

OLD SINGING GAME

The Muffin Man

OLD SINGING GAME

Did You Ever See a Lassie?

OLD SINGING GAME

las - sie do this way and that? Do this way and that way, Do

this way and that way; Did you ev - er see a las - sie Do this way and that?

The Mulberry Bush

OLD SINGING GAME

Brightly

1. Here we go round the Mul - berry Bush, The Mul - berry Bush, the Mul - berry Bush;
2. This is the way we clap our hands, We clap our hands, we clap our hands;
3. This is the way we wash our hands, We wash our hands, we wash our hands;
4. This is the way we brush our hair, We brush our hair, we brush our hair;
5. This is the way we tie our shoes, We tie our shoes, we tie our shoes;
6. This is the way we run a - way, We run a - way, we run a - way;

Here we go round the Mul - berry Bush, So ear - ly in the morn - ing.
This is the way we clap our hands, So ear - ly in the morn - ing.
This is the way we wash our hands, So ear - ly in the morn - ing.
This is the way we brush our hair, So ear - ly in the morn - ing.
This is the way we tie our shoes, So ear - ly in the morn - ing.
This is the way we run a - way, So ear - ly in the morn - ing.

Round and Round the Village

OLD SINGING GAME

Gaily

1. Go round and round the vil - lage, Go round and round the vil - lage, Go
2. Go in and out the win - dows, Go in and out the win - dows, Go
3. Now stand and face your part - ner, Now stand and face your part - ner, Now
4. Now fol - low me to Lon - don, Now fol - low me to Lon - don, Now

round and round the vil - lage, As we have done be - fore.
in and out the win - dows, As we have done be - fore.
stand and face your part - ner, And bow be - fore you go.
fol - low me to Lon - don, As we have done be - fore.

Can You Show me How the Farmer?

OLD SINGING GAME

Allegretto

Can you show me how the far-mer, Can you show me how the
far-mer, Can you show me how the far-mer Sows his bar-ley and wheat?

Yes, I'll show you how the far-mer, Yes, I'll show you how the
far-mer, Yes, I'll show you how the far-mer Sows his bar-ley and wheat.

London Bridge

OLD SINGING GAME

Allegretto

1. Lon-don Bridge is fall-ing down, Fall-ing down, fall-ing down!
2. Build it up with i-ron bars, I-ron bars, i-ron bars!
3. I-ron bars will rust and break, Rust and break, rust and break!
4. Build it up with sticks and stones, Sticks and stones, sticks and stones!
5. Sticks and stones will soon fall down, Soon fall down, soon fall down!

Lon-don Bridge is fall-ing down, My fair la-dye!
Build it up with i-ron bars, My fair la-dye!
I-ron bars will rust and break, My fair la-dye!
Build it up with sticks and stones, My fair la-dye!
Sticks and stones will soon fall down, My fair la-dye!

The Ring

By permission of The Thomas Charles Company

J. W. ELLIOTT

Allegretto

We chil-dren form a flow-er-y ring, And in the cir-cle dance and sing; Not
one of us goes in or out, On-ly the blue-bell turns a-bout.

VIII. MISCELLANEOUS

The Field Daisy

Anonymous

Edward B. Birge

I'm a pret-ty lit-tle thing, Al-ways com-ing with the Spring; In the mead-ows green I'm found, Peep-ing just a-bove the ground; And my stalk is cov-ered flat, With a white and yel-low hat.

My Shingle Boat

Agnes Choate Wonson

W. Otto Miessner

I launched my shin-gle boat to-day, And lest it might be blown a-way, I tied a string a-round it tight, So it could not sail out of sight.

Extremes

JAMES WHITCOMB RILEY

MARSHALL BARTHOLOMEW

A lit - tle boy once played so loud, da, da, da, da, da, da, da, da,

Boom! Boom! Boom! That the thun - der up in a thun - der cloud,

da, da, da, da, da, da, da, da, Boom! Boom! Boom! Said, "Since I can't be

heard, Why then, I'll nev - er, nev - er thun - der a - gain;"

da, da, da, da, da, da, da, da, Boom! Boom! Boom!

pp delicato

And a lit-tle girl once kept so still, *(fingers on lips)* **ppp** **mf** That she

heard a fly on the win-dow sill, *(fingers on lips)* Whis-per and say to a

la - dy bird, "She's the still - i - est child I ev - er heard!" *(fingers on lips)* *sempre pp*

Fiddle and I

LINN MOORE MILLER

LINN MOORE MILLER

Brightly

We'll sing of the days that are hap - py and glad, We'll

sing of the sun - ni - est weath - er; I draw on the strings and my

fid - dle it sings; Just fid - dle and I to - geth - er!

The New Bonnet

AGNES CHOATE WONSON

MABEL E. BRAY

I have a new bon-net with gay flow-ers on it; I'll wear it to-mor-row, if pleas-ant the day. I have a new bon-net With gay flow-ers on it; I hope that to-mor-row will be a fine day!

Little Betty Blue

TRADITIONAL

W. OTTO MIESSNER

Lit-tle Bet-ty Blue, lost her hol-i-day shoe; What will poor Bet-ty do? What will poor Bet-ty do? Why give her an-oth-er, to match the oth-er, And

then she will walk with two, And then she will walk with two.

Little Fishes

LINN MOORE MILLER

LINN MOORE MILLER

Simply

Lit - tle fish - es in the sea, Where it's deep, deep,
Lit - tle fish - es in the sea, Far a - way, a -

deep; And the si - lent moon-beams creep; Do you sleep, sleep, sleep?
way; Does a lit - tle morn - ing ray, Tell you when it's day?

Ten Pretty Maidens

TRADITIONAL

W. OTTO MIESSNER

Allegretto

A - round the green grav - el The grass grows so green, And ten pret - ty

maid - ens are fit to be seen. Wash them in milk, Dress them in

silk, And the first to go down shall be mar - - ried.

* This is a circle game with all players squatting down at the last phrase.

My Zither

Carol Powell

Old Italian Song

I have a lit-tle zith-er, It is with me all the day,____ And
when my toil is o-ver, Such mer-ry tunes I play.____

The Wind Mill

Nursery Rhyme

W. Otto Miessner

Blow, wind, blow!____ The wheels must go,____ Grind-ing flour from the farm-er's
wheat;____ Then the bak-er will take it, Will knead it and bake it, And loaves of good bread we shall
eat;____ And loaves of good bread we shall eat.____

Robin

Now the Time Has Come For Play

OLD RHYME   GERMAN FOLK SONG

Now the time has come for play; Let the lead-ers show the way.

Ev-'ry-bo-dy in a row; Left foot for-ward, off we go.

Baby Doll

MABEL E. BRAY   MABEL E. BRAY

I love my Ba-by Doll the best, She talks and shuts her eyes;_____ She

turns her head and bends her arms, And when I pinch, she cries.——

Sunset

VIRGINIA BAKER   CHARLES L. SCHULER

Slow the sun now sinks from sight; Soon for us it will_ be night;

For-eign coun-tries far_ a-way—— While we sleep are hav-ing day.

Mouse Cousins

Christina Rossetti

Moderato

The cit - y mouse lives in a house; The gar - den mouse lives in a bower; He's
The cit - y mouse eats bread and cheese; The gar - den mouse eats what he can; We

friend - ly with the frogs and toads, And sees the pret - ty plants in flower.
will not grudge him seeds and stalks, Poor lit - tle tim - id fur - ry man.

Polly's Piano

Moderato

Pret - ty keys, all black and white, Christ - mas brought for my de - light;

Lit - tle tunes on you I play, Tunes that sweet - er grow each day.

The Silk Worm

Rebecca B. Foresman

Moderato

Here's a bus - y lit - tle spin - ner Work - ing hard to earn her din - ner,

I am sure she nev - er guess - es What be - comes of all her dress - es.

The Star

THE MODERN MUSIC SERIES

Quietly

O star that climbs the west-ern sky, At twi-light ev-'ry day,_____ When dol-lie goes to sleep, and I must put my toys a-way._____

The Reason Why

TRANSLATED FROM THE GERMAN   GERMAN FOLK SONG

Brighly

1. Once there was a lit-tle fel-low Gai-ly dressed in
2. Once a lit-tle crim-son clo-ver Used to hear this
3. "Tell me," said the lit-tle clo-ver, "Why you sing the
4. "That's my song of thanks for man-y Dai-ly gifts of

gold-en yel-low; Zum, zum, zum, zum, Zum, zum, zum, zum, Was his song.
jol-ly ro-ver; Zum, zum, zum, zum, Zum, zum, zum, zum, All day long.
same song o-ver; Zum, zum, zum, zum, Zum, zum, zum, zum, Thro' the hours?"
sweet-est hon-ey, Zum, zum, zum, zum, Zum, zum, zum, zum, From the flow'rs,"

Buttercups

ANNA M. PRATT   J.P.CRONHAMM

Moderato

But-ter-cups can al-ways tell wheth-er we love but-ter well;

If we don't or if we do But-ter-cups will tell us true.

Sonata in D
(Running)

FRANZ JOSEPH HAYDN

Marche Heroique
(March)

FRANZ SCHUBERT

Sonatina
(Walking, Curtsy)

ROBERT SCHUMANN

Gavotte
(Running, Whirling
Leaves or Snowflakes)

FRANÇOIS J. GOSSEC

Military March

FRANZ SCHUBERT

Turkish March
From the Sonata in A Major

Wolfgang Amadeus Mozart

Cradle Song

EDVARD GRIEG

Gavotte

CHRISTOPH W. VON GLUCK
From the Ballet "Don Juan"

Soldiers' Chorus

Giuseppe Verdi
From "Il Trovatore"

Minuetto

George Frederick Handel

Original version

Minuet
From Symphony in B♭, № 12

Franz Joseph Haydn

D. C. al Fine

La Cinquantaine

GABRIEL-MARIE

Northern Song

Greeting to the composer, Gade

ROBERT SCHUMANN

Valse

FREDERIC CHOPIN

Carmen's Castanet Song

GEORGES BIZET
From "Carmen"

Ciribiribin

A. Pestalozza

Roses from the South
(Second Strain)

Johann Strauss

March of The Three Kings
(The Magi)

OLD FRENCH CHRISTMAS CAROL

Andante

LUDWIG van BEETHOVEN
From the Sonata "Pathétique"

Confidence

FELIX MENDELSSOHN

Theme from Sonata

Wolfgang Amadeus Mozart

Slumber Song

Robert Schumann

Mazurka

Frederic Chopin.

PART THREE

GENERAL SUGGESTIONS

I. Introduction

Music has always been recognized in the kindergarten as an essential means of achieving group-spirit. Charming and interesting to the children, it plays a vital part in leading them easily into group-play and in making their earliest class-experiences bright and happy ones. Even though a child may have sung and listened to music at home with his parents, the pleasure of singing, playing, and listening with others of his own age is a new experience and generally a thrilling one.

The authors of this book have endeavored to provide the teacher with material through which she may utilize the natural social tendencies of little children, such as play, imitation, and various types of physical activities. This material is on the mental and emotional level of the kindergarten and first-grade child. It includes songs relating to experiences and activities within the common observation of the children, such as those of the home, household occupations, pets, toys, and friends, and leads into the broader community life and activities. Songs are also included which arouse and satisfy the child's imagination, some songs which may cultivate a sense of humor, as well as many of a purely poetic character.

By the end of the kindergarten year the children should find pleasure in participating in rhythmic play, in singing, in dramatizing some of the songs and rhythms, and in listening to music. They should also have gained some ability to express rhythms in bodily movements, to play rhythm band instruments with the group, and to sing simple songs.

At the end of the first grade these outcomes should be along the same lines, but broader. Although skill is here a secondary consideration, the children should sing more easily and in better tune; should dramatize their songs and rhythms more freely and with increasing creative expression; should play the rhythm band instruments more rhythmically and with growing discrimination; and should show greater pleasure in listening to music, as well as in all of their other musical activities.

II. Singing

1. The voice of the child. The voice of the little child is extremely fine and delicate, and should have no strain whatever put upon it. The quality of the true "child-voice" is high and thin. It is not heavy or low. The singing voice of a child is his "head-voice." Many children have never sung a "head-tone" before they come to school. When they try to sing, they use either the "chest-voice" or the speaking voice. Parents say, "My child cannot sing high." No child can sing high with a "chest-tone."

The idea that children in kindergarten cannot be taught to sing well has been disproved. There is much very lovely singing in the kindergartens where the teachers themselves can sing and know how to catch the singing voices of the children. Also the old conception that the singing of little children must at first be heavy and unpleasant in quality has fortunately given way to a new idea that singing is putting into beautiful tone the thought that is to be expressed.

Even the smallest children enjoy hearing the teacher when she sings to them with sweet tones. "Birds sing sweetly and so do we!" "What a beautiful song-story this is!" The desire to express the thought of a lullaby or prayer will in itself help the children to make that expression beautiful. Harsh, ugly singing must have no place in school.

Wrong conceptions of singing which children often acquire from radio, movies, and adult singing must be counteracted by the best examples that can be had in school. Teachers must be trained to sing with lovely tone and clean diction, in contrast to the raucous crooning and harsh adult singing heard elsewhere by the children.

2. The "non-singers." Nearly all "non-singers" may be grouped in one of three classes:

(a) Those who have not yet found their singing voices.

(b) Those who are inattentive to pitch, or who do not yet recognize differences in pitch.

(c) Those who still lack coördination of the vocal muscles.

A bad ear is very rare, and is usually caused by some physical disability, such as defective speech, tongue-tied condition, partial deafness, adenoids, etc. A fourth classification includes those children who may have physical defects. These should be treated by medical specialists and should not be required or even allowed to try to sing unless so advised by the physician.

The First Group

All children should be treated at first on the supposition that they belong to the first class; *i.e.*, that they have not yet found their singing voices. As is stated above, the singing voice of a child is his head-voice, and most children have never sung a head-tone before they come to school. It is very easy, generally, to show a child where his head-voice is. Of course, the *teacher* must have the idea herself and must be able to produce a good tone. There are many simple devices of which the following are intended only to be suggestive:

Note: These "games" should be used as play in connection with the topic of the day, such as "birds," or the song being taught, such as "Bow-wow-wow!" page 4.

(1) Imitate "tweeting" of birds, or the cry of a little mouse, very high (G or F). Sing "Nee-nee-nee" on the same tones.

(2) Sing "Bow-wow-wow" on the same high tones, "barking" like a very small dog. Sing higher and higher. Change to "meow" and sing as high as possible. "Who can be the littlest kitten?"

(3) Imitate other animals and fowl. Always give a high pitch for starting.

(4) Imitate winds: "Whee-whee," very high. "Who can make the sound of the very smallest, highest winds?" "Oo-oo!" Make it very soft and high.

(5) Playing violins: Sing "me" very high and imitate motion of playing violin. Form an "orchestra" of those who play best. Competition always helps.

(6) Blow bugles on high F, F-sharp, and G, then down to C, third space. "Toot-toot-toot!"

(7) Ring bells: Begin high. "Ding-dong!" "Who has the highest, clearest, sweetest bells?" Orchestra of bells.

(8) Imitate street venders: Begin high. "Apples, Apples! Nice bananas!" etc.

(9) Sing phrases of words on one high tone.

(10) Play echo: Teacher sings; children echo. Good singer sings; class echo. Good singer sings; poor singer echo.

The above devices, and many others which will suggest themselves from the use of these, are the best "voice training" for the first months of school, for the good singers as well as the poor. The head-voice will be "caught" easily in this way, with most of the children. No child should be allowed to sing with a heavy, throaty tone.

The Second Group

The children of the second group (those who are inattentive to pitch) not only do not know the use of their head-voices, but also do not respond entirely to the above given devices. These children must first be given the *idea of up and down.* In the beginning all the children should be treated as belonging under the first class. Then those who after a reasonable time do not seem to notice "high" and "low" should be helped in other ways   This must always be done individually.

(1) *Motion up and down with hand* as teacher sings up and down.

(2) *Stand on toes*, to sing "up high."

(3) *Play games:*

(a) Teacher sings two words; child tells which is higher.

(b) When another child sings high, the non-singer jumps; when he sings low, the non-singer runs, etc., etc.

(4) *Marks put on board by teacher:*
Child points to high one and sings high, etc.

(5) *Games with toy instruments:*
Teacher strikes triangle and bells; child tells which is higher.
Teacher contrasts other instruments in the same way.

(6) *Teacher uses "guessing games"* in which children guess which instrument they hear. Also they should tell which sounds a higher tone, etc.

(7) *Teacher often uses piano for wide difference* in pitch. Compare extremely high and low tones. (A reed organ may also be used for this pitch discrimination.)

(8) *The Story of the Three Bears* has been found peculiarly effective in calling the attention of the children to differences of pitch. The teacher will find various ways to use this story. For instance, the teacher may be the father bear, a child (a good singer) the mother bear, and the child who is being helped the baby bear. The teacher will think of many variations.

Games catch the attention of all children and make for helpful competition. A good singer playing with one who is inattentive to pitch will help very much, but care should be taken that the good singer does not contract bad habits from the poor singer. Poor singers should sit near the teacher.

The Third Group

The children of the third group (those who still lack coördination of the vocal muscles) are harder to reach than the second, but after all do not present an impossible problem. To play with the other children in their "music games" is a great incentive. A few devices will suggest others for those children who still lack the coördination of the vocal muscles necessary to *make* the tone they *hear*.

(1) *Child puts hand up as high as he thinks the tone is*, thinking very hard, then sings "Bow-wow-wow" on that same tone.

(2) *Child moves hand up and down as teacher sings*, then puts hand up high and sings what the "hand says to do."

(3) *Child marks on board up and down* (one tone at a time) as teacher sings.

(4) *Child moves hand up and down while other children sing*, but does not sing.

(5) "*Thinks tone that teacher sings.*" Sings "Meow" on it. "Does it sound like the high 'meow' that the teacher sang?"

(6) *Child goes to piano*, plays a tone; *thinks* it; sings it. "Was it right?"

Great concentration of thought is necessary to overcome the difficulties of the children of this group, and that is impossible at their age except for a moment at a time. These children must have individual instruction until they begin to improve.

The "Non-Singer" Who Does Not Readily Respond to These Devices

There are *very few* such children. A few special devices may be used to help the stubborn cases, but the teacher will be able to find those that suit the individual better than any general ones that can be suggested.

(1) *Pinch the nose at the bridge:* "Feel the tone buzz." (Vibrations are felt.) Sing "Nee-nee-nee."

(2) *Hold the hand on top of the head:* "Feel the tone." Try to "tweet" like a very little bird.

(3) *Hold the ear against the piano:* Teacher plays a high, then a low tone. Child tells which is high. (He usually calls it "faster.")

(4) *Child strikes a gong:* Sings sound it makes. (Usually feels the vibrations.)

(5) *Child builds a scale of blocks:* Takes off top block, sings as each one is taken off. *Trying* helps to train the ear.

Individual instruction is absolutely necessary for these children. They must always listen when the other children sing. When they themselves sing with the others they get nothing, and they ruin the singing of the others.

Voice Training

All of the suggestions given above are excellent voice training studies and games. It is essential to insist upon a *high tone*, light in quality and easily sung. No heavy or loud singing should be allowed. There are many songs throughout the book which have refrains to be sung by "the non-singers." All "voice training" should be given in the spirit of play, and in connection with some activity which motivates the voice game.

3. The choice of songs. Because of the many considerations which go into the selection of songs for little children, it has not been feasible to arrange the songs in The Music Hour in the Kindergarten and First Grade in a graded plan. For most purposes it seemed best to use topical classifications, leaving the specific selection of songs to the teacher, who understands the degree of skill of her class and the classroom situation for which she will use the songs.

In the beginning, when "catching" the singing voices of the children is of paramount importance, the teacher will find the "refrain-songs" very helpful and interesting to the children. Carried along by pleasure in hearing the teacher sing, the children quickly learn to join in singing the refrain. A partial list of this type of song is suggested:

Page 7 Ironing Day (Children sing "Rub away!")
Page 15 Children, Good-by
Page 32 My Pony (Children sing "Gallop, a-gallop, a-gallop")
Page 36 The Duck and the Hen (Children sing "Quack, quack, quack" and "cluck, cluck, cluck")

Page 37   Three Little Kittens
Page 37   The Little Red Hen
Page 39   The Balloon Man
Page 105   When Cats Get Up
Page 107   The Telephone
Page 123   Autumn and Winter Winds
Page 124   Snowflakes
Page 154   The Big Drum
Page 155   Fiddles and Horns
Page 156   The Child and the Sparrow
Page 170   The Reason Why

There are numerous "sentence songs" throughout the book which will naturally be chosen by the teacher for use during the early part of the year, or for the development of less musical children. Some examples of this type of material are suggested:

Page 3   Playing with Baby
Page 4   Bow-wow-wow!
Page 8   Who's at the Door?
Page 12   Call to Work or Play
Page 15   A Good-by Song
Page 16   Riding
Page 16   Follow the Leader
Page 17   To Market
Page 23   Knock at the Door
Page 30   Puss
Page 32   The Merry-Go-Round
Page 37   Mooley Cow Red
Page 58   Fluttering Leaves
Page 61   January
Page 66   Baby Buds
Page 72   Kris Kringle's Travels
Page 76   Our Flag
Page 79   A, B, C, tumble down D
Page 80   Jack Be Nimble

The songs in The Music Hour in the Kindergarten and First Grade are presented in keys and compasses suitable for the voices of the children. The topics of the songs will often suggest "tone games" which the resourceful teacher will use daily in helping the children to "catch" their singing voices.

The teacher is referred to the topical index at the back of this book, not only in order that she may find songs suitable for the units of study in which the class is engaged, but also in order that she may find suggestions for amplifying and expanding the various phases of interest in these units.

4. How to teach songs. Throughout the kindergarten and first grade the children should sing as many songs as they are able to learn. This of course will vary with different classes, and will vary also because of the differences in the ability of the teachers. The idea that kindergarten children cannot learn to sing well even a few songs is as incorrect as the idea that all the songs of the daily routine must be sung by them. True, the children should learn as many as they can, and they should sing correctly those that they do sing. However, they should hear many more songs than they learn, and the teacher should be able to sing these songs to her class. Great differences in ability will be found in children from different sections of the same town, as well as in different classes of children in the same building. Early in the year the teacher will often have to sing to the children the very songs which later, with the development of their singing powers, they will be able to sing by themselves. Just as children learn to talk by hearing their parents speak, so they learn to sing by hearing the teacher sing.

Even though immediate results are not always apparent, these small children are acquiring the singing idea, and most of them will soon begin to sing not only the songs expected of them, but also those used by the teacher for enriching their listening experiences and for brightening the school day.

Music is here provided which suits the growing experiences of the children, following a natural outline of social life. The children are regarded as individuals, and the songs are particularly chosen with the thought that each child will make use of them to the extent of his desire and ability, at school and at home.

It is no longer an accepted idea that little children should learn the words of a song, as a poem, before learning to sing them to the melody. As a matter of experience, it has been found that this procedure produces "non-singers" rather than singers.

No song should be taught to kindergarten children that is too difficult either in length, in vocabulary, voice requirement, melody-line, or rhythm. If the song is right in these respects, there is no reason why the children should not learn it easily. The difficulty of teaching songs to little children often lies not so much with the children as with the teacher herself, and with the songs which she tries to teach. If the teacher cannot sing well and if she does not know how to "catch" the singing voices of her children and apply them to song singing, the unfortunate children in her class will surely be deprived of the chance to learn to sing. And alas! if they do not learn to sing, they learn not to sing. Those who expect to teach kindergarten or first grade should study piano and singing, and should also make a study of the child voice.

Two Ways of Teaching a Song

When children first come to school, they have generally had little experience with music, but they have a natural rhythmic sense, to which the first appeal should be made. Beginning with the very first song, the teacher's singing should be so rhythmic that the children's natural reaction will take the form of some motion suggested by the spirit of the song. At first, the children will only listen, but after they begin to feel the rhythm, they will do what the music says; as, for instance, "rock the baby." Later the song with accompaniment is played on the piano, while the teacher and children move to its rhythm. For several days the teacher may play or sing the song in connection with some phase of class activity. These preliminary steps in the presentation of rote songs are especially important in the kindergarten or with beginners in the first grade. When the children show by their attitude that they are beginning to know the words and that they have entered into the spirit of the song, it will be the signal for teaching it to them.

Whole-Song Procedure

The teacher sings, "Rock-a-Bye," page 2, while the children listen.

The children tell the teacher that the song is about rocking the baby to sleep.

The teacher sings the song again as rhythmically as she can, suggesting with her arms the motion of the mother rocking the baby.

The teacher sings the song and asks the children to rock the baby.

Later in the day, during a rest period, the teacher plays "Rock-a-Bye" on the piano.

Another Day:

The teacher hums "Rock-a-Bye," and asks the children what it is about.

The teacher plays it on the piano, or hums it again, and asks the children to show with their arms what the song says.

The teacher sings the song with words, while the children rock the baby.

The teacher plays or sings the song later in the day during a rest period.

Perhaps Another Day:

The teacher hums the song and asks the children to think the story.

When some of the children try to sing the song with her, she chooses the phrase best known (usually, of course, the first phrase), and asks the class to sing that phrase.

She may ask one child to sing what he knows, choosing a child who has tried to sing with her.

The teacher sings the phrase and all the children sing it with her. She then sings the entire song and the children who remember it sing with her. The children who do not remember the entire song sing as much as they can.

The teacher teaches those parts which the children do not sing well.

The teacher and the children sing the entire song.

A child who knows it sings the entire song.

The teacher and the children sing the entire song with accompaniment.

"Can you sing this Rock-a-Bye song to mother tonight? How about singing it to the baby? Who has a baby at home? Who knows a baby near by? Tomorrow we will see how many sang the song to mother and how many sang it to a baby!"

First grade children who have not attended kindergarten are vocally much the same as kindergarten children. For the first few months the Whole-Song Procedure is appropriate for these first grade children, and it may also be used during the first few weeks with children who have attended the kindergarten.

Phrase-wise Procedure

After the children have had considerable experience with the Whole-Song Procedure, they are ready for training that gives somewhat more definitely the phrase-structure of the songs that they learn. The following outline is suggested for use at a time when the teacher feels that the children are ready for this more advanced experience.

Teaching "My Baby-Bo," page 97

Teacher sings entire song as beautifully as she can.

She discusses the words, so that all the children understand them.

Teacher sings song again. She asks children to tell meaning of the words by phrases.

Teacher sings entire song again, with "loo," and children sway arms.

Teacher sings first phrase with words.

Children sing first phrase with words.

Teacher sings second phrase with words.

Children sing second phrase with words.

Teacher sings first and second phrases with words.

Children sing first and second phrases with words.

Teacher sings third phrase with words.

Children sing third phrase with words.

Teacher sings fourth phrase with words.

Children sing fourth phrase with words.

Teacher sings third and fourth phrases with words.
Children sing third and fourth phrases with words.
Teacher and children try entire song.
Teacher goes back to first phrase and sings. Children imitate. The teacher will stop to drill on any figures that trouble the children. These phrases are a bit long, and probably will need to be divided for drill. As quickly as possible the teacher asks the children to sing the entire song alone.

"When you go home, sing the song to mother and the baby. Tomorrow we shall see whether you remember it. Be sure to sing it with a lovely tone when you sing it at home.

"Tomorrow I am going to let some of you sing the song all alone for *us*. Won't that be lovely?"

Outline for the Next Day's Lesson

Teacher hums "My Baby-Bo"; children recognize it.
Teacher sings song with words; children move arms in rhythm.
Teacher sings song phrase-wise; children imitate.
Teacher and children sing entire song.
Children sing entire song, teacher not singing but leading with motion of her hand.
Teacher and children sing entire song with accompaniment, if possible.
Some of the individual children may sing with the accompaniment.

5. When to use the piano with singing. The piano should not be used by the teacher in teaching a song, but should be used in connection with a song in the following ways:

(1) After the teacher has sung the song without accompaniment, in order to give the children a clear idea of the words and melody, she may then sing it with its accompaniment.

(2) The teacher may play the song while the children listen, either to recall the song as something they have heard, or merely to suggest a mood.

(3) The teacher may play the song while the children rest, not expecting any particular response or reaction from them.

(4) After the song has been well learned by the children, the teacher may play the accompaniment while she and the children sing the song.

(5) The children should frequently sing without the piano and should never become dependent upon it.

NOTE: Most of the piano accompaniments in this book are very simple and the melody is prominent in nearly all cases. These accompaniments should be played softly, never dominating the children's singing. Some teachers like to play the melody only, either as written or an octave higher, as an aid in keeping the voices high and light. The accompanist should be cautioned to use the pedal sparingly.

6. Dramatization. The dramatic element of an activity is its most vivid quality in its appeal to children. Little children enter into any imaginative, or "make-believe" situation, carrying it on even beyond the point anticipated by the teacher. There should be many opportunities for this kind of expression, and music offers an attractive means of participation in imaginative play.

Little children easily imagine themselves an infinite variety of characters, both animate and inanimate. A child can be a bird, an elephant, the wind, a tree, the moon, or any other character which his fancy directs. Moreover, when he has become the imaginary person or thing, he spontaneously assumes the character with perfect seriousness and the utmost delight.

Numerous songs in The Music Hour in the Kindergarten and First Grade will appeal to this imaginative instinct of the child. In singing the song he should be encouraged to feel that he is the character itself, and that he is living the song's story. For example, "My Pony" on page 32 provides an excellent opportunity for the children to be ponies; and "Jack-in-the-Box," page 17, suggests its own activity. On page 23, "Two Little Blackbirds" suggests a little story where two children play together (nearly everybody knows the little game where a piece of colored paper is put on the finger nails and made to appear and disappear as the hand is lifted while singing the song). "On the Way to School," page 109, is a song-story which children delight to dramatize. Among the many songs which suggest their own activity, a few may be mentioned:

Page 7	Ironing Day
Page 11	Before School
Page 16	Playing in the Band
Page 26	My Fire Engine
Page 29	Wee Ducky Doddles
Page 45	I Am the Wind

The teacher should have no difficulty in finding a song of this nature for almost any occasion. Further suggestions for dramatizations of the songs in the book will be found under section VI, Operettas.

7. Songs to be sung to the children (but not to be sung by them). The statement was made above that the children should hear more songs than they are asked to sing, and that the teacher should be equipped vocally and musically to sing many songs beautifully to her class. These songs may be of several types:

(1) Songs from The Music Hour which the children in her class may not be ready to sing, but which illustrate the topic being developed at the time.

Suggestions:

Page 1   Autumn Leaves
Page 2   Morning
Page 3   Trot, Trot
Page 4   The Sandman
Page 5   Bunny
Page 11 Safety First
Page 25 Sleeping Dolls
Page 38 Piggy-wig and Piggy-wee
Page 47 The Sun
Page 47 The Wishing Star
Page 53 The Dragon
Page 63 Making a Snow-Man
Page 66 April Rain

These songs may be used by the teacher to illustrate a topic in hand, or for other appreciative purposes, although the children may never learn to sing them. There is not time enough for the children to learn all the songs which should be used, and it seems better to hear the more difficult ones and to learn only the simpler.

(2) Songs from The Music Hour which the children are not ready to sing at that time but which they will learn a little later.

Suggestions:

Page 9   The Cupboard
Page 13   Things I Like
Page 16   Playing in the Band
Page 17   Jack-in-the-Box
Page 23   Two Little Blackbirds
Page 24   Dolly's Lullaby
Page 97   Rockaway Land
Page 99   Cradle Time
Page 102 Work and Play
Page 103 Good Night
Page 111 The Delicatessen Store
Page 115 On the Bus
Page 116 The Aeroplane
Page 118 The River
Page 118 The Sea
Page 119 A Sea Song from the Shore
Page 126 The Dressed-Up Town
Page 128 Spring
Page 131 Butterfly and Honeybee
Page 133 Pansies
Page 136 The Mocking Bird
Page 137 The Oriole's Nest
Page 143 In Fairyland
Page 145 The Dove
Page 155 Fiddles and Horns

Page 162 Extremes
Page 163 Fiddle and I
Page 164 The New Bonnet
Page 164 Little Betty Blue

(3) Standard songs, some of which are listed below, which, like the standard pictures they see, will leave an impression of beauty in the minds of the children. This experience may be referred to or perhaps definitely used in some later year. Such songs become memories of beautiful music, sometimes to be recalled long afterward in some concert hall.

LIST OF STANDARD SONGS

Title	Composer
Slumber Song	Mozart
Lullaby	Brahms
When Children Lay Them Down	Schumann
The Little Dustman	Brahms
Sweet and Low	Barnby
The Slumber Boat	Gaynor
When the Little Children Sleep	Reinecke
Butterfly	Schumann
Spring's Messenger	Schumann
The Star	Schumann
Greeting	Mendelssohn
Barnyard Song	Grieg
Jerushy	Gaynor
Salute to the Flag	Gaynor
The Cuckoo Clock	Grant-Schaefer
The Doll's Cradle Song	Reinecke
The Postillion	Taubert
French Nursery Songs, from "Chansons Vieilles et Rondes," edited by Charles Marie Widor, and "Chansons de France," by J. B. Weckerlin	
Songs from "Art Song Cycles"	Miessner
Selections from "Songs of the Child World"	Riley and Gaynor

(A musical teacher will find many other suitable song classics.)

All the teacher's singing to the children should contribute decidedly to the background of music appreciation which is being built up for them. In some cases, records may be used to give the children the opportunity to hear certain songs as sung by artists. However, it is the teacher's own singing which makes the greater impression upon the children in the kindergarten.

8. Songs for aural observation. Before completing the work of the first grade, many classes will be ready to begin a more specific study of tone relations as found in some of the familiar rote songs.

As an introductory step, the teacher leads the children to observe the difference between ascending and descending passages. The next step is to observe songs in which the children listen for obvious repetitions and contrasts of phrases. While often undertaken in the latter part of the first grade, many teachers prefer to postpone this study until the second grade, just before beginning the work of The Music Hour, First Book.

This observation of tone relations should never become formal or mechanical. It should always be in the same spirit of play that has prevailed throughout the music lesson up to this point.

Further lessons in Aural Observation may be given according to the outline which follows.

Songs appropriate for this type of work are called "Rote Songs for Aural Observation," and are given in this book, Part Two, section IX, page 167, for use in first grade classes where this type of study is introduced.

Suggested Procedure

Lesson One. Aural Observation

Teacher's Aim:

To lead the children to discover, through listening, the phrase repetition and melody line of this song.

Situation:

(a) The children have learned many songs by rote, phrase-wise. They know the term "phrase" and understand its general meaning from their experience in learning rote songs.

Procedure

Teacher sings the song, "Robin," page 167.
Children discuss words.
Teacher tells children that today they will play a new game. She will sing the song, and they will listen to find how many phrases there are.
Teacher sings the song.
Children discover that there are four phrases.
Teacher says that she will sing again, and asks children to name any phrases that sound alike. Perhaps someone will hear how the music moves up and down.
Teacher sings the song as many times as is necessary.
Children discover that there are four phrases; that the first and third phrases are alike; that the second and fourth phrases are nearly alike; that the song starts on a high tone and moves downward; that the song ends on a low tone; and that each phrase ends with a long tone.

Lesson Two. Rote Presentation

After the previous lesson the children will almost know the song. However, the teacher should not take this for granted, but should teach it as she would teach any rote song.

Lesson Three. Review of Phrase Study

Procedure

The teacher sings the song, "Robin," with "loo."
Children recognize the song.
Teacher recalls phrase repetition.
Teacher: "Let us sing the song again, you singing the first phrase, and I the second, you the third phrase, and I the fourth."
This is done, all singing with "loo."

At this point the lesson may be varied in a number of ways by singing phrases by alternate rows, different individuals, etc. The teacher may point to the phrase marks on the board or may have different children do so.

The teacher should use her ingenuity to make this lesson as interesting as possible to the children by presenting it in the spirit of a game. The lesson should end by singing the song with "loo," then with words.

Lesson Four. So-fa Syllables (optional)

If the teacher thinks it wise, she may at this point teach the *so-fa* syllables by rote, as she would teach another stanza to the song. Many teachers prefer to delay this step until the second grade.

III. Rhythm Play

The development of a strong feeling for rhythm is one of the most desirable outcomes of experience in music. On the other hand, a well-developed sense of rhythm is a fundamental attribute for musical feeling. Most music educators are in agreement that the sense of rhythm is best developed through physical activity. Expression of rhythmic feeling in bodily movement is natural to children, and many opportunities for this response should be provided among their first music experiences. The imagination of some children will lead them to spontaneous dramatizations, while others may sway to the rhythm, or dance, or may merely listen with pleasure. One child's response will often stimulate and suggest activities to other children.

Free and creative responses in the rhythmic play of the first two years lead naturally to a more organized expression which is gradually developed through free rhythmic play, singing games, and dances in succeeding years.

Another allied field of rhythmic activity, *The Toy Orchestra*, or *Rhythm Band*, is treated in a later section.

The instrumental music for rhythmic play and free dramatic interpretation was chosen with the thought of contributing directly to the child's appreciation of music. The selections are standard compositions which the children will be glad all their lives to have learned in their first years of school.

1. **Impersonation.** Under section II, "Singing," dramatization and impersonation were suggested in connection with the stories of many of the songs. It was suggested that the children should live the song. These impersonations would naturally tend to fall into rhythmic expression, following the rhythmic feeling of the song. In connection with the development of rhythmic feeling, the teacher should also offer opportunities for interpretations of a directly rhythmic nature. The term "dramatization" naturally refers to songs where the words give the clue to the activity. In addition, however, The Music Hour in the Kindergarten and First Grade offers a large number of delightful instrumental selections for free rhythmic expression and interpretation, as for example:

Page 28   The Elephant
Page 29   The Bear
Page 30   The Rabbit
Page 31   Sparrows Hopping
Page 34   Circus Parade

2. **Directed activities.** An additional type of rhythmic response is suggested by such activity songs as the following:

Page   3   Trot, Trot
Page   3   Playing with Baby
Page 10   Cradle Song
Page 16   Follow the Leader
Page 17   To Market
Page 18   Playing Ball
Page 19   A Game
Page 24   The Rocking Horse
Page 32   My Pony
Page 40   The Young Engineer
Page 44   The Carpenters
Page 48   Little Raindrops
Page 58   Fluttering Leaves
Page 68   Tap, Tap, Tap!
Page 78   Dickory, Dickory, Dock
Page 104   Gray Pony
Page 113   The Busy Cobbler
Page 154   The Big Drum

In this classification also are the instrumental selections for which an activity is suggested, such as:

Page 86   The Wild Rider (Galloping)
Page 172   Gavotte (Running and Whirling)

3. **Free response.** Among the obviously appropriate responses for children of this age are: walking, running, trotting, galloping, hopping, stepping, whirling, gliding, clapping, tapping, throwing, sawing, etc. The title of the selection, as well as the varying rhythmic and melodic character of the music, will suggest to the children varying moods and mood contrasts. For example, "The Flatterer" (Butterfly), page 84, suggests an entirely different mood from that of "Evening Prayer," page 92.

Some variations that stimulate interest and assist in associating the action with the rhythms and character of the music may be listed: fast and slow, soft and loud, stepping high, walking through fallen leaves, walking through deep snow, tripping like fairies, striding like giants, stalking like elephants, dancing like bears, marching like a band, following a leader, forming several lines with leaders, stepping side-wise, jumping rope, skating, rowing, and different forms of impersonation and imitation.

4. **Creative expression.** After the children have had experience in dramatizing some of their songs and in expressing the rhythms of some of the instrumental selections, it will contribute to their growth and pleasure if they are offered opportunities to express themselves in original activities as suggested by the music. The value of this depends upon the extent to which the teacher allows the children freedom of expression and to which it does not become a reflection of the teacher's own ideas. Too often children are asked to offer original interpretation before their experience has provided them with a vocabulary of expression. The following selections are examples of compositions which permit true creative response:

Page 48   The Brook
Page 49   The Lake
Page 62   Snowflakes
Page 64   Spring Song
Page 64   Melody in F
Page 67   Invitation to the Dance
Page 124   Snowflakes

The teacher will find suggestions for further types of activities in "Creative School Music," by Lillian Mohr Fox and L. Thomas Hopkins, published by Silver Burdett Company.

5. Traditional singing games. Another application of the principle of rhythmic development is that of traditional games, such as:

Page 16   Follow the Leader
Page 158   Did You Ever See a Lassie?
Page 158   Looby Loo
Page 158   The Muffin Man
Page 159   The Mulberry Bush
Page 159   Round and Round the Village
Page 160   London Bridge

These games not only offer opportunities for varied rhythmic activities, but they are a definite step toward the development of group consciousness.

IV. Music Appreciation

Since music is used so generally to accompany every phase of the day's activities, there is here a challenging opportunity for developing true music appreciation. This implies the ability to enter freely into rhythmic interpretation, to sing beautifully in the true spirit of the song, to listen with pleasure, and to follow the mood or story of the music. Every piece of music that he hears, every song that he sings, and every selection which he interprets rhythmically or dramatically should contribute actively to the child's appreciation of good music.

The mood appeal of music begins when little children notice the difference between a march and a lullaby. The contrast of major and minor almost always brings to them a very decided change of mood. Children will soon distinguish mood variations in music through listening to the "fairy music." The music of the elves, brownies, and good fairies, which is dainty, sweet, and happy, will be contrasted with that of the witches, goblins, gnomes, etc., which is weird, harsh, and unhappy. Songs about autumn winds contrast sharply with those about spring flowers or birds.

The approaches to music appreciation in the kindergarten and first grade may be given as follows:

(1) *Singing.* The songs should be sung as beautifully as possible, with every effort to produce a good tone quality and clear pronunciation of the words. The children should be taught to sing the song with attention to the flow of phrases, and to recognize the phrase as an element of song. They should be led to recognize also rhythmic differences as expressive of different moods and ideas. The spirit of the song, expressed by the words, should be reflected in the tone quality, the rhythmic accentuation, and the tempo.

(2) *Rhythm Play.* Through motor responses to the rhythm of the music the child becomes an actual part of the music which he recreates by his activity. By means of dramatizations he also identifies himself with the composition. This leads directly into a keener appreciation of the music.

(3) *The Toy Orchestra.* The ways in which the toy orchestra contributes to music appreciation are discussed in detail under "The Toy Orchestra."

(4) *Listening.* The listening lesson should aim to present music clearly related to the child's own familiar moods and experiences. The children are familiar with the idea of a lullaby, for instance. By hearing a number of selections expressing this idea they become aware of the power of music to express the mood of a lullaby. This is true also in relation to other childish experiences, such as marching, imitating fairies and animals, and expressing other phases of their imaginative life.

The following classified list of recorded compositions is offered as a suggestion to the teacher in selecting material in addition to that in the book, illustrative of the various topics of the year.

TOPICAL ASSIGNMENT FOR KINDERGARTEN AND FIRST GRADE

	No.
Animal and Fowl	
The Bee — Schubert	20614
Of Br'er Rabbit — MacDowell	22161
Art Songs to Be Sung to Children	
Songs for Children — Grant-Schaefer — Riley-Gaynor	20738
Art Song Cycles — Miessner	20441
Cycle of Seasons	
Snowballing (La Czarine) — Ganne	20430
Spring Song — Mendelssohn (See II–III)	20195
Fairy World	
Caprice — Ogarew	20614
The Fairies — Gaynor	20738
Gnomes — Reinhold	19882
In the Hall of the Mountain King — Peer Gynt Suite — Grieg	20245
Minute Waltz (Happy Fairies) — Chopin	20614
The Witch — Tschaikowsky, and Elfenspiel — Kjerulf	20399

Holidays and Festivals
Adeste Fideles, Nazareth, The First Nowell   20174

Moods
Aloha Oe — Hawaiian, and From the Land of the Sky-
    Blue Water — Cadman   1115
Adeste Fideles   20174
Badinage — Herbert, Humoresque — Dvořák, Minuet —
    Beethoven   20164
Believe Me, If All Those Endearing Young Charms —
    Irish, and Stars of the Summer Night — Woodbury . . .   21938
Caprice — Ogarew   20614
Minuet in G — Paderewski   20169
Old Folks at Home — Foster, and Home, Sweet Home —
    Bishop   4001
Sweet and Low — Barnby, and Rock-a-bye Baby —
    Traditional   20174
Waltz, No. 2 — Brahms   20162

Mother Goose
Songs for Children   20212

Nature
To a Water Lily, and To a Wild Rose — MacDowell . . .   22161
Wind Amongst the Trees — Briccialdi, and At the Brook —
    Boisdeffre   20344

Play, and Rhythm Play
Andante "Surprise" Symphony — Haydn (See IV–V) . . .   7059
Anitra's Dance — Peer Gynt Suite — Grieg   20245
Boating on the Lake — Kullak   20401
Gavotte — Popper   20164
Knight of the Hobby-Horse — Schumann   20399
Lullaby — Brahms, and Rock-a-bye Baby — Traditional . .   20174
Marionnettes — Glazounow   20914
Minuet — Paderewski   20169
Mirror Dance — Gounod, and Peasants' Dance — Schytte   20399
Omaha Indian Game Song   20164
Persiflage — Francis   20914
Run, Run, Run — Concone   20162
Spinning Song — Kullak, The Little Hunters — Kullak,
    The Wild Horseman — Schumann   20153
Turn Around Me   21620
Waltz in A flat — Brahms, Skaters' Waltz — Waldteufel,
    Minuet — Mozart, Amaryllis — Ghys   21938

Story in Music
Of a Tailor and a Bear — MacDowell   20153
Postilion — Godard, The Clock — Kullak   20399

Toy Orchestra
Legend of the Bells — Planquette   20164
Menuet in G — Bach (See II–III)   1136
Minuet — Mozart   21938
Rendez-vous — Aletter, and La Czarine — Ganne   20430
Turkish March — Mozart (See II–III)   1193
Waltz in A flat — Brahms, Amaryllis — Ghys, Skaters'
    Waltz — Waldteufel   21938

*(The following additional records, not appearing in The Music Hour
minimum list, on page 209, have been found useful by many teachers throughout the country.)*

Barcarolle — Tales of Hoffman — Offenbach   20011
Dance of the Chinese Dolls — Christmas Tree Suite —
    Rebikov   22163
Entrance of the Little Fauns — Pierné   22163
Hurdy-Gurdy Man, The — Kaleidoscope — Goossens . . .   21945

Liebesfreud — Old Vienna Waltz — Kreisler   8285
March — Aïda — Verdi   22764
Rataplan — Daughter of the Regiment — Donizetti . . .   22169
Shadows — Schytte   22169
Waltz in D flat — Minute Waltz — Chopin   20614
With Castanets — Reinecke   22169

V. The Toy Orchestra

In order to make the children ultimately conscious of music as something interesting and important in their lives, and to lead them to discover and feel music as something through which they may express themselves, it is necessary to make many contacts through the play spirit during the first two years in school. The toy orchestra is a delightful approach to music appreciation, as well as a direct means of stimulating an interest in instrumental music, particularly an interest in orchestral instruments. At first the rhythm band was thought by teachers to be only a phase of rhythmic training, but as the children used the instruments the music teacher came to realize that the toy orchestra has larger values and that much more than rhythm sensing and expression can be developed from this popular activity. The term "Toy Orchestra," therefore, is used to suggest gradual addition of instruments of varied tone qualities and definite pitch.

The emphasis on rhythmic development in the kindergarten and first grade is on activities involving the whole body and belongs primarily in the field of rhythmic activities as outlined in section III of these teaching directions. Although toy orchestra experience has definite rhythmic values, these values lie more particularly in the appreciative field, wherein phrases and meters and rhythmic contrasts should be emphasized. Also the toy orchestra has special values in developing discrimination of tone qualities appropriate for the expression of varied moods and for contrasting sections of compositions.

The standard selections in Unit XIV, page 87, in Unit XI, page 173, and in the recorded selections listed on page 209, for kindergarten and first grade toy orchestras, will lay a foundation for music understanding and appreciation through playing, as well as through listening and singing.

The Instruments

If the toy orchestra is to contribute to the music appreciation of the children, it is necessary that instruments of good quality be used. The best toy instruments or even good semi-professional instruments will be found to repay fully the extra expense. Inexpensive instruments of the better kind are now being made and sold for school use.

A good balance of tonal effect is essential to the success of the toy orchestra. The following grouping will be found satisfactory for a class of thirty children:

> 2 bird whistles
> 3 triangles
> 4 pairs jingle bells
> 4 pairs jingle sticks
> 2 tambourines
> 1 pair cymbals
> 1 Chinese wood-block
> 1 maple bar xylophone
> 3 pairs sand blocks
> 8 pairs rhythm sticks
> 1 drum

Seating Plan

Drum

Xylophone   Cymbals

Tambourines   Jingle Sticks

Bells   Sand Blocks   Wood Blocks

Triangles   Bird Whistles   Rhythm Sticks

Leader

Playing the Selections

In the kindergarten quite a little time will need to be occupied in becoming acquainted with the instruments and in learning to handle them. Resourceful teachers find ways of accomplishing this which will give pleasure to the children and not lessen their interest. The children should call the instruments by name, and each should handle them all in turn. A game may easily be made of this study of the instruments, and the children will feel that they know what is going on when they play together. After the teacher finds which children can best handle the different instruments, selections should be played by the entire group together, in order that the group-playing may be rhythmic. The children are not yet ready to work out any particular effects; it is easier now for them to play all the time. Marches are particularly good for this "unison" playing, as are the little minuets and other dances offered in this book for that purpose.

The sensing of different rhythms and their expression through unison playing will occupy most of the first year. The playing of the children should be spontaneous always, and the spirit of fun should prevail. Team-work which will result from playing together is a strong factor in developing group-consciousness and a spirit of play. Toward the end of the year some of the children may be ready to notice differences in mood effects and may want to express these in their playing. It is possible then to give these particular children certain sections of the pieces to play as they wish. Often they want to use the soft-toned instruments only, in some passages, and to contrast these with the heavier instruments. They may feel that some passages should be played more slowly. These phases of toy orchestra playing, which may start in the kindergarten and which will surely develop in the first grade, provide a real approach to music appreciation.

Some teachers believe that the playing of familiar songs offers a more practical approach to toy orchestra than beginning with longer instrumental selections. Suggested instrumentation for two such songs will be found on page 202, "Greeting to Visitors," and "Old Mother Wind."

Another interesting use of the toy orchestra will occur in such songs as "The Dressed-Up Town," page 126, and "A Sea Song from the Shore," page 119, where the orchestra may play the dance which follows the singing.

The music for the toy orchestra in this book is marked phrase-wise by number. The possibilities for the orchestration of each selection may thus easily be studied by the teacher before she presents the music to the children.

Suggested Instrumentations for Kindergarten

Finale from Sonata in D, by Haydn, page 87

Use only the following instrumentation: Rhythm sticks, triangles, bells, jingle sticks, sand blocks, tambourines, and wood block. Play in unison, making the first and second phrases (as numbered in the book) quite soft, the third, fourth, and fifth slightly louder, the sixth loud, and the seventh softer. Repeat in the same way to *Fine*.

Minuet from "Don Juan," by Mozart, page 88

When first introduced, all instruments play this together in unison, as suggested for the preceding selection, and use only soft-toned instruments. This is a rather slow movement. Play the (1) and (2) softly, the (3) with more tone, and the (4) softly.

Near the end of the year, or in the first grade, the complete instrumentation given on page 198 will be found practical and effective.

Little Minuet in G, by Bach, page 88

Do not use the heavier instruments with this at first. At the beginning of the year, allow all the children to play in unison. Show the children playing tambourines, jingle sticks, and bells how to shake their instruments, and give them a signal to play in this manner where a shake is indicated (∿). This will give a dainty effect, which the children like. The teacher should study the music and assist the children in noting where the softer passages occur.

Later in the year, or in the first grade, the instrumentation given on page 199 will be enjoyed by the children.

The other selections on pages 89, 90, and 91 should first be played in unison, with the aim of helping the children to play rhythmically together, and to lead them to feel the rhythm and some of the variations in volume of tone, which are easily noticeable if the pianist plays well. Some classes may be able to do more than is suggested here, but it has been found that most children of kindergarten age need and enjoy much experience in these fundamentals of toy orchestra playing.

Suggested Instrumentations for First Grade

After the first grade children have recalled their experiences with the toy instruments and have played together some of the familiar selections of their kindergarten days, they should be encouraged to assist in choosing the instruments which they think are appropriate to the mood and spirit of the different portions of the music. The teacher should study the music as to the possible instrumentation and as to the effects which she feels she could get with the children's playing. She can then decide upon the appropriateness of different instruments as they are proposed by the children for the different sections of the music.

On the following pages will be found suggested instrumentations for several of the selections appropriate for playing in the first grade. These instrumentations are given in different styles of notation and with different symbols as developed by teachers in various parts of the country. They are for the guidance of the teacher and are not intended to be used by the children. As the class develops instrumentations for other selections, the teacher may find it helpful to use one of these plans of scoring in order to remember from time to time the way in which the instrumentation has been planned.

The first three instrumentations are of the type used by Miss Mabel E. Bray, Director of Music, New Jersey State Teachers College, Trenton, New Jersey. The instrumentations on pages 202–204 were prepared by Miss Florence R. Stumpf, Director of Music Education, Hillsborough County, Florida. The instrumentations on pages 205–207 were worked out by classes under the direction of Dr. Lena Milam, Director of Music, Beaumont, Texas.

THE TOY ORCHESTRA

Key to Instrumentation

R.S. — Rhythm sticks
Tr. — Triangle
Tam. — Tambourines
B — Bells
WB — Wood block
Bl. — Plain blocks and sand blocks
    (Unless otherwise indicated)

S.B. — Sand blocks only
G — Gong
Xyl. — Xylophone
Cym. — Cymbals
Dr. — Drums
Birds — Bird whistle
J.S. — Jingle sticks

Directions and Code

Each instrument should play only where indicated by abbreviation
of name of instrument or the down stroke (') under beat.

Tr. means that the triangles play only on indicated beat.

R.S. means that the rhythm sticks play on respective beat and
thereafter when indicated by the sign (').

' means tap.

〰 means shake or roll.

SUGGESTED INSTRUMENTATIONS

Minuet, "Don Juan," by Mozart (see page 88)

Little Minuet in G, by Bach (see page 88)

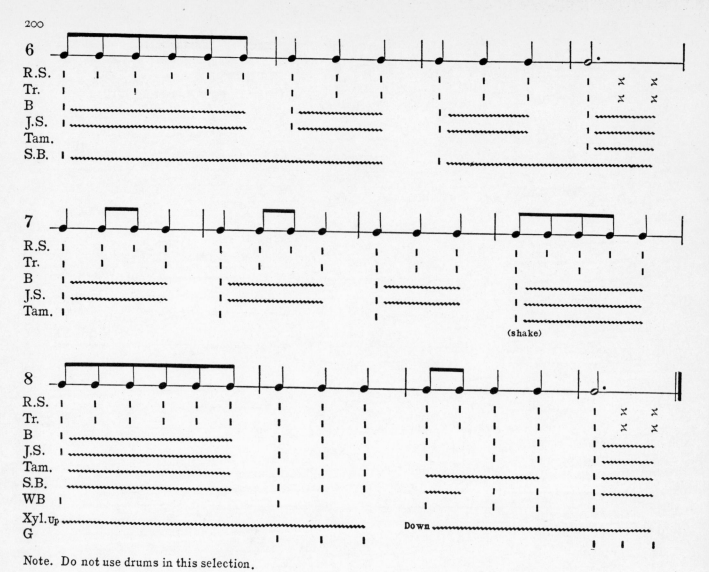

200

Note. Do not use drums in this selection.

Military March, by Schubert (see page 173)

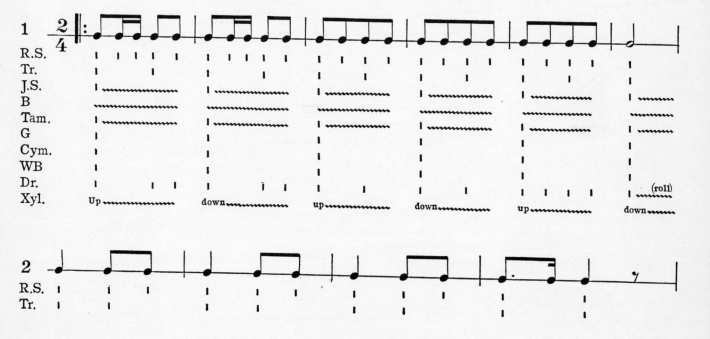

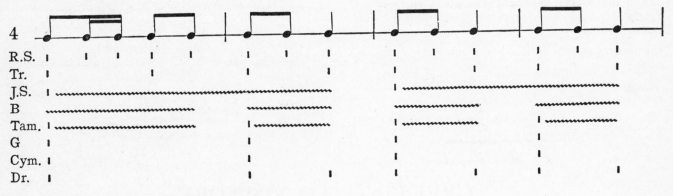

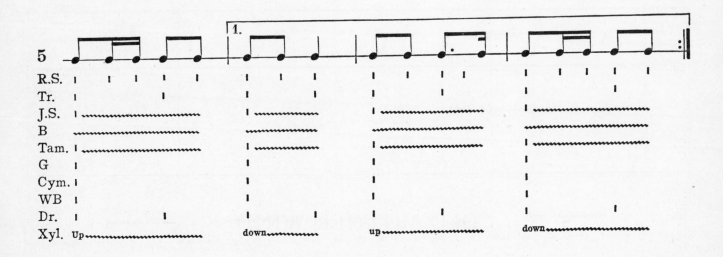

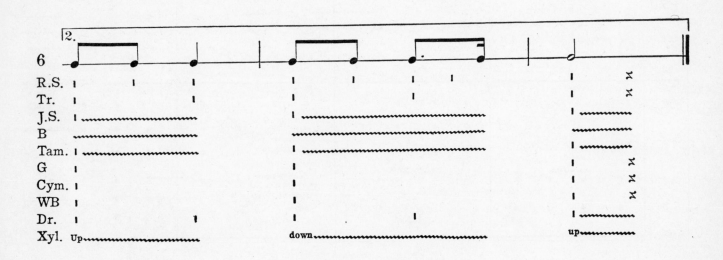

DIRECTIONS FOR PLAYING INSTRUMENTS AND SYMBOL NOTATION

<u>For rap of clog</u>—strike clog against palm of left hand.

<u>For tambourine rap</u>—hold left fist in position and rap tambourine <u>against</u> fist (instead of hitting tambourine with <u>motion</u> of fist).

∿∿∿continue shaking instruments.

〰 short shake.

The rhythm sticks should be held loosely in hand—struck lightly about one inch from end and drawn <u>instantly</u> apart after blow.

Instruments may be tucked under arm when not being used.

△ trill as close in top corner of instrument as possible. Strike a lower bar if possible.

• expressed by an outward movement of the hand, <u>away</u> from the instrument.

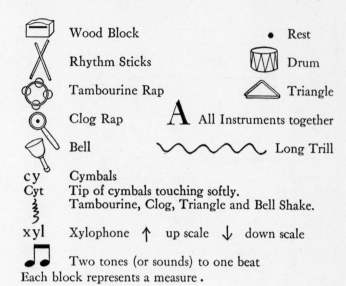

Wood Block	• Rest
Rhythm Sticks	Drum
Tambourine Rap	Triangle
Clog Rap	**A** All Instruments together
Bell	∿∿∿ Long Trill
cy Cymbals	
Cyt Tip of cymbals touching softly.	

Tambourine, Clog, Triangle and Bell Shake.

xyl Xylophone ↑ up scale ↓ down scale

♫ Two tones (or sounds) to one beat

Each block represents a measure .

GREETING TO VISITORS

Brightly *Arranged by* FLORENCE R. STUMPF

OLD MOTHER WIND

Quietly *Arranged by* FLORENCE R. STUMPF

RATAPLAN-DONIZETTI
Col. Record A 3130 or Victor 22169

Orchestration by FLORENCE R. STUMPF

SHADOWS-SCHYTTE

Arranged by FLORENCE R. STUMPF

Well accented

The Little Red Hen (see page 37)

Three Little Kittens (see page 37)

The Big Drum (see page 154)

Hey, Diddle Diddle (see page 80)

Playing Ball (see page 18)

Little Jack Horner (see page 78)

Little Bunny Rabbit (see page 140)

Brownies (see page 51)

The Candy Lion (see Second Book, page 14)

VI. Operettas

1. Informal musical plays. So many of the songs of this book are adaptable to dramatic arrangement around some central story that it is quite possible to make little informal plays for classroom use, and even to use these songs in the form of simple operettas.

Such little plays, or informal dramatizations, can be made by the children and the teacher without any preliminary drill, and may be "worked out" as they progress. Given the freedom to use their imaginations, pupils of this age will use a slender rod as a wand, transforming a little girl at once into a most beautiful fairy queen. An aviator's cap will change a little boy into a flyer with the daring of an "ace." The other children will enter into these flights of fancy, often adding to the spirit and color of the portrayal. No stage properties are necessary, but the children themselves will suggest how to use blocks, chairs, tables, and other pieces of furniture to heighten the effect of the play. For these classroom plays, the teacher and the children make the dialogue to fit the situations and to suit their ideas and desires.

Several subjects are here suggested, with a short list of songs which may be used as a basis for making the dialogue.

A Trolley Trip to the Park

The Trolley Car . . . . p. 41
The Traffic Light . . . . p. 44
The Traffic Cop . . . . p. 44
The Organ Man . . . . p. 39
The Drum . . . . p. 27
The Fire . . . . p. 40
In the Park . . . . p. 43
Pigeons . . . . p. 6

A Shopping Trip

The Candy Shop . . . . p. 112
The Five and Ten Cent Store . . . . . . p. 112
The Baker's Shop . . . . p. 112
Bread and Cherries . . . . p. 111
Buy . . . . p. 42
The Balloon Man . . . . p. 39

In Our City

The Trolley Car . . . . p. 41
The Flagman . . . . p. 40
The Postman . . . . p. 42
The Busy Postman . . . . p. 108
The Fountain . . . . p. 43
In the Park . . . . p. 43
The Carpenters . . . . p. 44
Newsboy . . . . p. 108
The Street-Cleaner Man . . . . p. 109
On the Way to School . . . . p. 109
The Trolley Man . . . . p. 110
On the Bus . . . . p. 115

The Birds' Party
(Use songs about birds and trees.)

The Tea Party

The Invitation   "Who's at the Door?" . . . p. 8
      "The Postman" . . . . . p. 42
Getting Ready   "The New Bonnet" . . . . p. 164
Going to Party   "Safety First" . . . . . . p. 11
At the Party   "At Tea" . . . . p. 9
      "Animal Crackers" . . . . p. 9
      "Politeness" . . . . p. 14
      "Friends for Tea" . . . . p. 101
Going Home   "The Motor Car" . . . . . p. 116

These dramatizations should be very free and informal, and should bring the songs into a still closer relation to child life. Such plays may be used for additional motivation in learning the songs. The teacher who has dramatic flair will give her children experiences which will feed their imaginative life and afford them much pleasure.

2. More formal operettas. A second type of dramatization is illustrated by the following little operetta. The story procedure is outlined by the teacher, and the thought of the dialogue also. But the wording and arrangement of the dialogue should be free, so that the children need not use the same lines each time. For instance, "Oh goody!" might be changed by the child to "Oh good!" or to "Goody! Goody!" or to "That's great!" That he expresses the joy he feels is the essential thing.

The operetta "Going to the Circus" is offered as a suggestion to the teacher who can do this sort of dramatization with her little children. The action should never be formal or "set," but free and varying, according to the children's interpretation. "The best way" might be agreed upon finally before a public performance. But even then the children should be free to do and say what will best express their idea.

Many other operettas may be made from the material in the book. The beautiful fairy music suggests "A Visit to Fairyland," etc., etc.

GOING TO THE CIRCUS

(For First Grade — Last Half)

The Plot

The circus parade and the street boys following make the children eager to go to see the animals and all the sights. Mrs. Moore agrees to take her three boys and three of their little friends to the circus. She takes them in her motor car.

When they reach the tent, the balloon man is outside, and they each buy a balloon. The organ man is playing his hurdy-gurdy near by. A merry-go-round is also seen. The children enjoy all of them.

The band plays and it is time to go inside. The animals interest the children; one likes the monkey best, another the bear, another the elephant, another the ponies. One likes the circus folks. The parade is repeated inside the tent. At last it is time to go home.

Outside the tent the candy man is selling candy. A newsboy is there, too, selling papers. An airplane sails by. The children and Mrs. Moore get into the car and start for home. They see a traffic cop and a traffic light. When they arrive home, they play circus with father. The operetta closes at bed time.

The Characters

Mrs. Moore, the mother, who conducts the circus party
John, Benny, and Bub, Mrs. Moore's children
Betty, Nancy, and Peggy, friends of the Moore children
The Balloon Man
The Organ Man
The Merry-Go-Round Man
Manager of the Circus Parade
The Circus Folk
Monkey, Bear, Elephant, Ponies
Drummer and Orchestra, or Band
The Candy Man
Newsboy
Traffic Cop
Father (Mr. Moore)

This plan provides for about thirty children. There may be more or less.

Scene One

In the Moores' House

The Circus Parade is heard.
Benny: "Oh, mother, will you take us to the circus?"
John and Bub: "Oh, yes, mother!"
(The boys run to the window and watch the parade.)

THE STREET BOYS' PARADE, p. 22, is heard.

John: "Oh, see, the boys are all following the parade!"
Mrs. Moore: "Well, children, I think I must take you to the circus. Would you like to invite Betty and Nancy and Peggy?"
Boys: "Oh, goody!"
Mrs. Moore: "You run and ask the girls if they can go, while I get out the car."
(Boys run off, and Mrs. Moore goes for the car.)

Scene Two

In the Car

The children come back and find mother in the car.
Sing: "The Auto," p. 41. (The stanza may be changed to:
"Climb into the auto.
We're off for the day
To see the big circus
And hear the band play.")
Children chatter freely, having a gay time.
Bub: "Mother, see the light! It is red."
All sing "The Traffic Light," p. 44 (also might sing "The Motor Car," p. 116).
Betty: "Here we are! Oh, see the balloons!"
(All get out of car.)

Scene Three

Outside the Tent

Balloon Man sings "The Balloon Man," p. 39.
All sing "The Balloon Man."
Mrs. Moore: "How do you do, Mr. Balloon Man! We all want balloons. Choose your colors, children."
(The children choose. Each has a gay balloon.)
Nancy: "Oh, I love to hear the organ man play. I'm going to give him a penny."
(Organ man plays, and then thanks the children for their pennies.)
All sing "The Organ Man," p. 39.
John: "The circus isn't open yet. Let's ride on the merry-go-round."
(The Merry-Go-Round Man takes their money.)

All sing "The Merry-Go-Round," p. 32.
Benny: "There's the band! Now we can go in."
All sing "Playing in the Band," p. 16.

Scene Four

Inside the Tent

The circus parades around the tent.
Play "The Circus Parade," p. 34.
Some children take the parts of bears, elephants, monkeys, ponies, circus folks, and the band.
Peggy: "I like the monkey." Peggy sings "The Monkey," p. 33 (or all may sing).
Bub: "I like bears best." Bub sings "The Bear," p. 29 (or all sing). Play "The Bear," p. 29, while the bear dances. Children imitate.
Benny: "Here is the elephant! I like him best." Benny sings "The Elephant," p. 28. Play "The Elephant," p. 28. Children imitate the child who represents the elephant.
John: "The ponies are best, I think." John sings "My Pony," p. 32. Play "Happy Journey," p. 28. Children dramatize.
Nancy sings "At the Circus," p. 145.
All sing "At the Circus," p. 145.
Mrs. Moore: "Now we must go home. It is getting late. What a lovely time we have had!"
All go out.

Scene Five

On the Way Home

The Candy Man sings "Buy," p. 42.
Mrs. Moore: "Well, it is nearly supper time, but we'll buy some candy to eat for dessert."
Newsboy sings "Newsboy," p. 108.
Mrs. Moore: "Come, get into the car. We must hurry home."
John: "There's a traffic cop, mother."
All sing "The Traffic Cop," p. 44.
(They are now going into their driveway.)
Bub: "Oh, dear! the circus is over, and I'm hungry. Oh, here's father!"
Father asks where they have all been.
The children tell him about the circus.
Bub: "Oh, father, let's play circus after supper!"
Finale: All come forward.
Sing "Playing Circus," p. 17.
Sing "Bed Time," p. 104.

VII. List of Correlating Recorded Music

The minimum list of records is organized in four units:
K–I (Victor Unit E–21). Kindergarten and First Grade. (Correlating with The Music Hour in the Kindergarten and First Grade.)
II–III (Victor Unit E–22). Second and Third Grades. (Correlating with the First and Second Books and the Elementary Teacher's Book.)
IV–V (Victor Unit E–23). Fourth and Fifth Grades. (Correlating with the Third and Fourth Books and the Intermediate Teacher's Book.)
VI (Victor Unit E–24). Sixth Grade. (Correlating with the Fifth Book and the Teacher's Guide for the Fifth Book.)

VICTOR RECORD UNIT (K–I) TO ACCOMPANY THE MUSIC HOUR IN THE KINDERGARTEN AND FIRST GRADE *

No.	Title
1115	Aloha Oe — Hawaiian
	From the Land of the Sky-Blue Water — Cadman
	Kreisler
4001	Home, Sweet Home (Harp) — Bishop
	Old Folks at Home (Harp) — Foster
	Salvi
19882	Gnomes — Reinhold, Dwarfs — Reinhold
	Fairies (Scherzo) — Schubert, Clowns — Midsummer Night's Dream — Mendelssohn
	Victor Symphony Orchestra
20153	1. Of a Tailor and a Bear — *MacDowell* 2. The Wild Horseman — Schumann
	1. Spinning Song — Kullak 2. The Little Hunters — Kullak
	Victor Orchestra

* See RCA-Victor Manufacturing Company circular, "Units for Use with The Music Hour."

20162   1. Run, Run, Run — Concone   2. Jumping — Gurlitt   3. Running Game — Gurlitt   4. Air de Ballet — Jadassohn
Waltzes Nos. 1, 2, and 9 — Brahms

Victor Orchestra

20164   1. Badinage — Herbert   2. Legend of the Bells — Planquette   3. Humoresque — Dvořák   4. Scherzo from 3rd Symphony — Beethoven
  1. Minuet — Paderewski   2. Gavotte — Popper   3. Minuet — Beethoven   4. Omaha Indian Game Song — Kinscella

Victor Orchestra

20169   Minuet in G — Paderewski
Amaryllis — Ghys

Victor Concert Orchestra

20174   1. Rock-a-bye Baby — Traditional   2. Sweet and Low — Barnby   3. Lullaby — Brahms
  1. Adeste Fideles — Portugal   2. First Nowell — Traditional   3. Nazareth — Gounod

Victor Concert Orchestra

20212   1. Hey Diddle Diddle   2. Little Bo-Peep   3. Twinkle, Twinkle, Little Star   4. Little Jack Horner   5. See-Saw, Margery Daw   6. Ride a Cock Horse — Elliott
  1. A Dew Drop — Gilchrist   2. When the Little Children Sleep — Reinecke   3. Rain Song — Smith

Erva Giles

20245   Anitra's Dance — Peer Gynt Suite — Grieg
In the Hall of the Mountain King — Peer Gynt Suite — Grieg

Victor Symphony Orchestra

20344   Wind Amongst the Trees (Flute) — Briccialdi
At the Brook — Boisdeffre

Venetian Trio

20399   1. Mirror Dance — Gounod   2. Elfenspiel — Kjerulf   3. The Witch — Tschaikowsky   4. March of the Tin Soldiers — Tschaikowsky
  1. Knight of the Hobby-Horse — Schumann   2. The Clock — Kullak   3. Postilion — Godard   4. Peasants' Dance — Schytte

Victor Orchestra

20401   1. Boating on the Lake — Kullak   2. Skating — Kullak   3. Walzer — Gurlitt   4. March — Gurlitt
  1. La Bergeronette — Burgmüller   2. Waltz — Schubert   3. Scherzo — Gurlitt   4. L'Arabesque — Burgmüller   5. Tarantelle — Saint-Saëns

Victor Orchestra

20430   La Czarine — Mazurka — Ganne
Rendez-vous — Intermezzo — Aletter

Victor Salon Orchestra

20441   1. Granddaddy Long Legs — Miessner   2. Touching — Miessner   3. Katydid — Miessner
  1. In Scotland — Miessner   2. In China — Miessner   3. In Germany — Miessner

Edna Brown

20614   1. The Bee — Schubert   2. Waltz in D flat (Minute Waltz) — Chopin
Caprice — Ogarew

Schmidt

20738   1. The Sandman — Grant-Schaefer   2. Spinning Song — Grant-Schaefer
  1. Slumber Boat — Gaynor   2. The Top — Gaynor   3. The Fairies — Gaynor

Anna Howard

20914   Marionnettes — Glazounow
Persiflage — Francis

Victor Concert Orchestra

21620   Hewett's Fancy — English Folk Dance
Turn Around Me — Czecho-Slovak Folk Dance   2. Hansel and Gretel — Humperdinck

Victor Band

21938   1. Waltz in A flat — Brahms   2. Stars of the Summer Night — Woodbury   3. Believe Me, If All Those Endearing Young Charms — Irish Air
  1. Skaters' Waltz — Waldteufel   2. Minuet (Don Juan) — Mozart   3. Amaryllis — Gavotte — Ghys

Victor Symphony Orchestra

22161   1. To a Wild Rose   2. To a Water Lily — Woodland Sketches — MacDowell
  1. A Deserted Farm — Woodland Sketches   2. Of Br'er Rabbit — Fireside Tales — MacDowell

Myrtle C. Eaver

22620   Songs recorded from The Music Hour in the Kindergarten and First Grade
Kindergarten
  1. Playing Ball, p. 18   2. The Broom, p. 8   3. The Postman's Whistle, p. 42   4. The Traffic Cop, p. 44   5. Piggy-wig and Piggy-wee, p. 38   6. The Rocking Horse, p. 24   7. Brownies, p. 51   8. Old Mother Wind, p. 46   9. Wee Ducky Doddles, p. 29
First Grade
  1. On the Way to School, p. 109   2. A Sea Song from the Shore, p. 119   3. The Barber, p. 114   4. Sing, Said the Mother, p. 131   5. The Secret, p. 134   6. The Dressed-Up Town, p. 126

Anna Howard

25423   Songs recorded from The Music Hour in the Kindergarten and First Grade
Kindergarten
  1. Dame, Get Up, p. 8   2. Children, Good-by, p. 15   3. Two Little Blackbirds, p. 23   4. My Fire Engine, p. 26   5. Church Bells, p. 27   6. My Pony, p. 32   7. Taddy Pole and Polly Wog, p. 36   8. The Balloon Man, p. 39
  1. The Little Red Hen, p. 37   2. The Auto, p. 41   3. The Young Engineer, p. 40   4. Boating Song, p. 68   5. The Carpenters, p. 44   6. Who Likes the Rain? p. 141 (1st grade)

Anna Howard

25424   Songs recorded from The Music Hour in the Kindergarten and First Grade
First Grade
  1. Playing in the Band, p. 16 (Kindergarten)   2. Little Bunny Rabbit, p. 140   3. In Fairyland, p. 143   4. The Big Drum, p. 154   5. My Zither, p. 166

Anna Howard

CLASSIFIED INDEX OF SONGS AND INSTRUMENTAL COMPOSITIONS

TITLE	PAGE
Autumn Leaves	1

I. HOME AND AROUND THE HOME

Kindergarten

TITLE	PAGE
Animal Crackers	9
At Tea	9
Baby's Way, A	2
Bow-wow-wow!	4
Broom, The	8
Bunny	5
Clocks	10
Cradle Song	10
Cupboard, The	9
Dame, Get Up	8
Dish-Washing Song	5
Ironing Day	7
Morning	2
Now Good-Night	3
Pet Bird, The	6
Pigeons	6
Playing with Baby	3
Real Work	7
Rock-a-Bye	2
Sandman, The	4
Spinner, The	4
Time to Get Up	10
Trot, Trot	3
Washing Day	7
Who's at the Door?	8
Wise Little Gold Fish	6

First Grade

TITLE	PAGE
Ann's Teeth	98
Baby's Lullaby	98
Bed Time	104
Callers	101
Come, Let's to Bed	103
Cradle Time	99
Doggie's Bath	106
Friends for Tea	101
Funny Little Bunny	106
Good Night	103
Gray Pony	104
Happy Child, A	104
Housekeeping	100
Land of Counterpane, The	99
Looking-Glass Child, The	103
Mix a Pancake	100
Mother and Father	98
My Baby-Bo	97
My Dicky Bird	105
Oh, Here Is Miss Pussy	106
Rockaway Land	97
When Cats Get Up	105
When Daddy Comes Home	101
Work and Play	102

II. SCHOOL

Kindergarten

TITLE	PAGE
Before School	11
Call to Work or Play	12
Children, Good-by	15
Going to School in the Rain	14
Good-by Song, A	15
Good Morning!	13
Good Morning, Happy Children	13
Greeting to Visitors	15
Morning Prayer	14
Politeness	14
Ready for School	12
Right Way, The	13
Safety First	11
Things I Like	13

III. PLAY; GAMES AND PLAY ACTIVITIES

Kindergarten

TITLE	PAGE
Follow the Leader	16
Game, A	19
Jack-in-the-Box	17
Knight of the Hobby-horse	22
Knock at the Door	23
Little Waltz	18
March	20
Marching	21
Parade, The	21
Playing Ball	18
Playing Circus	17
Playing in the Band	16
Riding	16
See-Saw	23
Street Boys' Parade	22
To Market	17
Two Little Blackbirds	23
Waltz from "Love's Dream after the Ball"	19

First Grade

TITLE	PAGE
Big Drum, The	154
Can You Show Me How the Farmer?	160
Child and the Sparrow, The	156
Did You Ever See a Lassie?	158
Fiddles and Horns	155
London Bridge	160
Looby Loo	158
Muffin Man, The	158
Mulberry Bush, The	159
My Scooter	157
Nineteen Birds	156
Playing Indian	157
Ring, The	160
Round and Round the Village	159
Sing Me a Song	157
Swing Song	156
Yankee Doodle	154

IV. TOYS

Kindergarten

TITLE	PAGE
Church Bells	27
Dolly's Lullaby	24
Drum, The	27
My Fire Engine	26
My Flute	26
My Teddy Bear	26
Paper Dolls	24
Playing the Bugle	27
Rocking Horse, The	24
Sleeping Dolls	25
Whirl, Top, Whirl!	25

V. ANIMALS; IMITATING ANIMALS AND ABOUT ANIMALS AND FOWL

Kindergarten

TITLE	PAGE
Allegro in B♭	31
Arabesque	28
At the Zoo	32
Bear, The	29
Black Thief, The	36
Cat and the Dog, The	38
Circus, The	33
Circus Parade	34
Elephant, The	28
Duck and the Hen, The	36
Happy Journey	28
Lazy Cat, The	33
Little Red Hen, The	37
Merry-Go-Round, The	32
Monkey, The	33
Mooley Cow Red	37
My Pony	32
Pifferari, Les	30
Piggy-wig and Piggy-wee	38
Puss	30
Squirrel, The	31
Taddy Pole and Polly Wog	36
Theme from the "First Mazurka"	29
Three Little Kittens	37
Tin Soldiers and Pussy	30
Wee Ducky Doddles	29

First Grade

TITLE	PAGE
At the Circus	145
Baa, Baa, Black Sheep	142
Caterpillar	141
Dove, The	145
Five Little White Mice	144
Friendly Cow, The	141
Frogs at School	142
Gray Squirrel	139
Gray Squirrels	140
In Fairyland	143
Kitty White	138
Little Bunny Rabbit	140
My Dog	138
My Hen	143
Rabbit, A	139
Shear the Sheep	142
Waggley Dog, The	139
Who Likes the Rain?	141
Zoo, The	144

VI. COMMUNITY LIFE AND COMMUNITY ACTIVITIES

Kindergarten

TITLE	PAGE
Airplane, The	41
Auto, The	41
Balloon Man, The	39
Buy	42
Carpenters, The	44
Fire, The	40
Flagman, The	40
Forge, The	43
Fountain, The	43
In the Park	43
Organ Man, The	39
Postman, The	42
Postman's Whistle, The	42
Shoe the Old Horse	39
Traffic Cop, The	44
Traffic Light, The	44
Trolley Car, The	41
Young Engineer, The	40

First Grade

TITLE	PAGE
Aeroplane, The	116
Baker's Shop, The	112
Barber, The	114
Bread and Cherries	111
Busy Cobbler, The	113
Busy Postman, The	108
Candy Shop, The	112
Carpenters' Song, The	113
Concerning Travel	115
Delicatessen Store, The	111
Engines	115
Farmer, The	110
Fireman, The	107
Five and Ten Cent Store, The	112
Hurdy-Gurdy, The	108
If I'd as Much Money	114
Motor Car, The	116
Newsboy	108
Old Woman, The	110
On the Bus	115
On the Way to School	109
Street-Cleaner Man, The	109
Telephone, The	107
Town Clock, The	114
Trolley-Man, The	110

VII. NATURE AND SEASONAL; FORCES OF NATURE; CYCLE OF SEASONS

Kindergarten

TITLE	PAGE
April Rain	66
At the Seaside	49
Baby Buds	66
Baby Leaves, The	66
Beds	69
Beginning to Grow	65
Boating Song	68

VII. NATURE AND SEASONAL; FORCES OF NATURE; CYCLE OF SEASONS — *Continued*

TITLE	PAGE
Boats Sail on the Rivers	49
Brook, The	48
Caprice	60
Cherry Tree, The	69
Coasting	63
Crow, The	59

Cycle of Seasons

A. Autumn

Caprice (Birds Fly Away)	60
Crow, The	59
Fluttering Leaves	58
Four Seasons, The	58
Melody (Fall Things Blowing)	60
November	60
Signs of Autumn	58
Valse (Dancing Leaves)	59

B. Winter

Coasting	63
January	61
Making a Snow-Man	63
Mazurka Russe (Snowballing)	62
Poor Snow-Man, The	62
Snowbirds	61
Snowflakes	62
Which Way Does the Wind Blow?	61

C. Spring

April Rain	66
Baby Buds	66
Baby Leaves, The	66
Beginning to Grow	65
Fly, Kite	65
Melody in F (Spring Mood)	64
Spring Song	65
Spring Song	64

D. Summer

Beds	69
Boating Song	68
Cherry Tree, The	69
Invitation to the Dance	67
Summer Days	67
Summer Night	68
Tap, Tap, Tap!	68
Thirsty Butterfly	69

Fluttering Leaves	58
Fly, Kite	65
Four Seasons, The	58
I Am the Wind	45
In the Wood	50
Invitation to the Dance	67
January	61
Lake, The	49
Little Raindrops	48
Making a Snow-Man	63
Mazurka Russe	62
Melody	60
Melody in F	64
Moonlight	46
Mountain, The	50
Murmuring Zephyrs	45
November	60
Old Mother Wind	46
Poor Snow-Man, The	62
Rainy Day	48
Signs of Autumn	58
Snowbirds	61
Snowflakes	62
Spring Song	65
Spring Song	64
Storm, The	46
Summer Days	67
Summer Night	68
Sun, The	47
Tap, Tap, Tap!	68
Theme from the Sonata in A	50
Thirsty Butterfly	69
Valse	59
Which Way Does the Wind Blow?	61
Wishing Star, The	47

First Grade

Autumn and Winter Winds	123
Autumn Fires	122

TITLE	PAGE
Baby Birds	134
Bee, The	130
Birds	135
Bobolink, The	135
Brook, The	117
Butterfly and Honeybee	131
Clouds	120
Dressed-Up Town, The	126
Early Spring	129
Feeding the Birds	134
Gardener, The	132
I'd Like to Be a Farmer	123
Jack-in-the-Pulpit	129
January and February	127
Lady Daffadown	130
Leaves Are Gone, The	123
Leaves in Autumn	122
Lily Bells	135
Man-in-the-Moon, The	121
March	127
Mocking Bird, The	136
My Kite	120
North Wind Doth Blow, The	124
Oak Trees	133
Oriole's Nest, The	137
Owl, The	136
Pansies	133
Rain	117
Rain in April	129
Rain in Summer	130
River, The	118
Robin, The	132
Sea, The	118
Sea Song from the Shore, A	119
Secret, The	134
Ships	119
Sing, Said the Mother	131
Skating	125
Snowflake Feathers	126
Snowflakes	124
Snowman, The	125
Spring	128
Spring Flowers	128
Summer and Winter	122
Swinging	132
When the Stars	121
Willow Cats, The	127
Wind, The	120

VIII. FAIRY WORLD

Kindergarten

Album Leaf (Brownies' March)	55
Brownies	51
Dragon, The	53
Entr'acte Music (Quiet Fairies)	54
Fairies' March	53
Foreboding of Grief (Sad Fairies)	57
Giants, The	54
I Wish	51
Larghetto (Goblins)	57
Little Goblin, The	51
"Minute Waltz" (Happy Fairies)	56
Moonlight Scene (Fairies in Moonlight)	52
Nocturne (Fairies Asleep)	57
Stephanie Gavotte (Fairies' Dance)	55

IX. HOLIDAYS; FESTIVALS; CELEBRATIONS, AND SPECIAL DAYS

Kindergarten

Abraham Lincoln	74
Adeste Fideles (Christmas Procession)	73
Arbor Day	75
Baby's Birthday	77
Birthday Song	77
Christmas Chimes	71
Christmas Day	71
Christmas Song, A	72
Columbus Was a Sailor	70
Dancing Doll (Christmas Toys)	72
Dressed-Up Town, The	126
Easter-Time	75
For Our Soldiers	76
George Washington's Birthday	74
Hallowe'en Night	70

TITLE	PAGE
Happy New Year	74
Kris Kringle's Travels	72
May Day	76
Nazareth (For the Christmas Program)	73
Our Flag	76
Silent Night	74
Thanksgiving	71
Who'll Be My Valentine?	75

First Grade

America	153
Arbor Day Tree, An	152
Christmas Bells	150
Columbus	148
Easter Eggs	152
Flag Day	153
Hallowe'en	148
Lincoln	151
Making a Valentine	152
May Basket	153
Merry Christmas	149
New Year, The	150
Salute the Flag	148
Thanksgiving Day	149
Valentines	151
Washington and the Flag	151

X. MOTHER GOOSE

Kindergarten

A, B, C, Tumble Down D	79
Bobby Shafto	79
Dickory, Dickory, Dock	78
Hey, Diddle Diddle	80
Jack Be Nimble	80
Little Jack Horner	78
Little Miss Muffet	80
See-saw Margery Daw	79

First Grade

Hark, Hark, the Dogs Do Bark	147
Humpty Dumpty	146
King of France, The	147
Mary, Mary, Quite Contrary	146
Old King Cole	147

XI. RHYTHM PLAY

Kindergarten

Allemande (Jumping and Hopping)	83
Andante (Lightly Stepping)	82
Fair Land of Poland, The (March)	81
Flatterer, The (Butterfly)	84
Gipsy Rondo (Running)	82
Happy and Light of Heart (Skipping)	85
Malbrough Has Gone to War (Skipping)	85
March (Running)	83
March	82
Pirates' March	81
Variations on a French Melody (Hopping and Jumping)	84
Wild Rider, The (Galloping)	86

First Grade

Gavotte (Running, Whirling Leaves or Snowflakes)	172
Marche Héroique (March)	171
Sonata in D (Running)	171
Sonatina (Walking, Curtsy)	172

XII. SUGGESTED SELECTIONS FOR RHYTHMIC ACTIVITIES

Clapping

Clocks	10
Tap, Tap, Tap! (Woodpecker)	68

Free Expression

Caprice (Birds Fly Away)	60
Dancing Doll (Christmas Toys)	72
Dressed-Up Town, The	126
Moonlight Scene (Fairies in the Moonlight)	52
Murmuring Zephyrs (The Wind)	45
Sea Song from the Shore, A	119
Stephanie Gavotte (Fairies' Dance)	55

XII. SUGGESTED SELECTIONS FOR RHYTHMIC ACTIVITIES — Continued

TITLE | PAGE

Gliding

Skating 125

Hopping and Jumping

Allegro in B♭ (Sparrows Hopping) . . . 31
Allemande (Jumping and Hopping) . . . 83
Funny Little Bunny 106
Pifferari, Les (The Rabbit) 30
Squirrel, The 31
Variations on a French Melody (Hopping and Jumping) 84

Running

Flatterer, The (Butterfly) 84
Gipsy Rondo (Running) 82
March (Running) 83
Melody (Fall Things Blowing) 60
"Minute" Waltz (Fairies) 56
Sonata in D (Running) 171

See-Saw

See-Saw 23
Waltz from "Love's Dream after the Ball" 19

Skipping

Happy and Light of Heart (Skipping) . 85
Humpty Dumpty 146

Swaying

Baby's Lullaby 98
Boating Song (Rowing) 68
Broom, The (Sweeping) 8
Cradle Song 10
Dolly's Lullaby 24
Knight of the Hobby-Horse (Rocking) . 22
Rock-a-Bye 2
Rockaway Land 97
Rocking Horse, The 24
Sleeping Dolls 25
Swing Song 156
Swinging 132
Theme from the Sonata in A (Swaying Trees) 50

Throwing

Little Waltz (The Bouncing Ball) . . . 18
Mazurka Russe (Snowballing) 62
Playing Ball 18

Trotting and Galloping

Circus Parade 34
Gray Pony 104
My Pony 32
Wild Rider, The (Galloping) 86

Walking

Album Leaf (Brownies' March) 55

TITLE | PAGE

Andante (Lightly Stepping) 82
Arabesque (Elephants) 18
Big Drum, The (March) 154
Brownies 51
Circus Parade (Marching Elephants) . . 34
Drum, The 27
Entr'acte Music (Quiet Fairies) 54
Fair Land of Poland, The (March) . . 81
Fairies' March 53
Giants, The 54
Happy Journey (High Stepping Horses) . 28
I Wish (Fairy) 51
Little Goblin, The 51
March 82
March 20
Marche Héroique 171
Marching 21
Parade, The 21
Pirates' March 81
Sonatina (Walking, Curtsy) 172
Street Boys' Parade 22
Theme from the "First Mazurka" (The Bear) 29
Wee Ducky Doddles 29
Yankee Doodle 154

Waving Flags

Flagman, The 40
Our Flag 76

Whirling

Gavotte (Running, Whirling Leaves or Snowflakes) 172
Snowflakes 62
Valse (Dancing Leaves) 59

XIII. TOY ORCHESTRA

Kindergarten

Cradle Song 91
Finale from Sonata in D 87
Gavotte 89
Gavotte in D 90
Little Minuet in G 88
Minuet 88
Toreador Song 90
Turkish March 91

First Grade

Carmen's Castanet Song 179
Cinquantaine, La 178
Ciribiribin 180
Cradle Song 175
Gavotte 175
March of the Three Kings (The Magi) . 181
Military March 173
Minuet 177
Minuetto 176

TITLE | PAGE

Northern Song; Greeting to the Composer, Gade 178
Roses from the South (Second Strain) . . 180
Soldiers' Chorus 176
Turkish March 174
Valse 179

XIV. MOODS; TO BE PLAYED FOR THE CHILDREN

Kindergarten

Boat Song 93
Cradle Song 95
Cradle Song 92
Evening Prayer 92
Gavotte 94
Habanera 94
Largo 96
Minuet 95
O Tender Moon 93
Waltz, No. 2 96

First Grade

Andante 182
Confidence 182
Mazurka 184
Slumber Song 184
Theme from Sonata 183

XV. MISCELLANEOUS

First Grade

Extremes 162
Fiddle and I 163
Field Daisy, The 161
Little Betty Blue 164
Little Fishes 165
My Shingle Boat 161
My Zither 166
New Bonnet, The 164
Ten Pretty Maidens 165
Wind Mill, The 166

XVI. ROTE SONGS FOR AURAL OBSERVATION

First Grade

Baby Doll 168
Blossoms 167
Buttercups 170
Cherries Ripe 167
Mouse Cousins 169
Now the Time Has Come for Play . . 168
Polly's Piano 169
Reason Why, The 170
Robin 167
Silk Worm, The 169
Star, The 170
Sunset 168

ALPHABETICAL INDEX OF SONGS AND INSTRUMENTAL COMPOSITIONS

Selections on pages 1–96 are in the Kindergarten Section, and those on pages 97–184 are in the First Grade Section.

TITLE	AUTHOR OR SOURCE	COMPOSER OR SOURCE	PAGE
A, B, C, Tumble Down D	Mother Goose	Elliott	79
Abraham Lincoln	Bray	Bugle Call	74
Adeste Fideles		Reading	73
Aeroplane, The	Applegarth	Miessner	116
Airplane, The	Bray	Bray	41
Album Leaf		Grieg	55
Allegro in B♭		Mozart	31
Allemande		Couperin	83
America	Smith	Carey	153
Andante	Sonata "Pathé-tique"	Beethoven	182
Andante	"Surprise Symphony"	Haydn	82
Animal Crackers	Miller	Birge	9
Ann's Teeth	de la Mare	Miessner	98
April Rain	Wonson	Miessner	66
Arabesque		Karganoff	28
Arbor Day	Decker	Protheroe	75
Arbor Day Tree, An		Terhune	152
At Tea	Bray	Ambrose	9
At the Circus	Morgan	Terhune	145
At the Seaside	Stevenson	Miessner	49
At the Zoo	Clark	Protheroe	32
Auto, The	Hartford	Hartford	41
Autumn and Winter Winds	Bray	French	123
Autumn Fires	Wonson	Birge	122
Autumn Leaves	Turner	Terhune	1
Baa, Baa, Black Sheep	Mother Goose	Elliott	142
Baby Birds	Bray	French	134
Baby Buds	Anonymous	Birge	66
Baby Doll	Bray	Bray	168
Baby Leaves, The	Clark	Ambrose	66
Baby's Birthday	Wonson	Miessner	77
Baby's Lullaby	Burnham	Holt	98
Baby's Way, A	Hicks	Terhune	2
Baker's Shop, The	Chaffee	Findlay	112
Balloon Man, The	Garnett	Protheroe	39
Barber, The	Miller	Ambrose	114
Bear, The	Wonson	Findlay	29
Bed Time	Hartford	Hartford	104
Beds	Fox	Grant-Schaefer	69
Bee, The	Miller	Miller	130
Before School	Shepard	French	11
Beginning to Grow	Wynne	Terhune	65
Big Drum, The	Douglas	Seely	154
Birds	Wonson	Protheroe	135
Birthday Song	Thompson	Protheroe	77
Black Thief, The	Clark	Miessner	36
Blossoms	Anonymous	Bray	167
Boat Song		Gounod	93
Boating Song	Applegarth	Modern Music Series	68
Boats Sail on the Rivers	Rossetti	French	49
Bobby Shafto	Mother Goose	Miessner	79
Bobolink, The	Clark	Miessner	135
Bow-wow-wow!	Mother Goose	Traditional	4
Bread and Cherries	de la Mare	Rogers	111
Brook, The		von Gluck	48
Brook, The	Fassitt	Mueller	117
Broom, The	Watkins	McConathy	8
Brownies	Thompson	Protheroe	51
Bunny	Thompson	Protheroe	5
Busy Cobbler, The	Applegarth	Ware	113
Busy Postman, The	Bray	English	108
Buttercups	Pratt	Cronhamm	170
Butterfly and Honeybee	Miller	Miller	131
Buy	Mother Goose	Russian	42
Call to Work or Play	Bray	French	12
Callers	Decker	Birge	101
Can You Show Me How the Farmer?		Singing Game	160
Candy Shop, The	Miller	Miller	112
Caprice	"Alceste"	von Gluck	60
Carmen's Castanet Song	"Carmen"	Bizet	179
Carpenters, The	Hartford	Hartford	44
Carpenters' Song, The	Hartford	Hartford	113
Cat and the Dog, The	Nursery Rhyme	Bray	38
Caterpillar	Wonson	Mueller	141
Cherries Ripe	English	English	167
Cherry Tree, The	Watkins	Ware	69
Child and the Sparrow, The	Westwood	Grant-Schaefer	156
Children, Good-By	Miessner	Miessner	15
Christmas Bells	Bokeloh	Bliss	150
Christmas Chimes	Old Song	Christmas Song	71
Christmas Day	Bray	Protheroe	71
Christmas Song, A	Baker	McConathy	72
Church Bells	Bray	Swedish	27
Cinquantaine, La		Gabriel-Marie	178
Circus, The	Pratt	Mueller	33
Circus Parade		Mueller	34
Ciribiribin		Pestalozzi	180
Clocks	Bray	Bray	10
Clouds	de Lorenzi	Mueller	120
Coasting	Hartford	Hartford	63
Columbus	Bray	Spanish	148
Columbus Was a Sailor	Thompson	Protheroe	70
Come, Let's to Bed	Mother Goose	White	103
Concerning Travel	Hofman	Grant-Schaefer	115
Confidence		Mendelssohn	182
Cradle Song	Traditional	Traditional	10
Cradle Song		von Wilm	91
Cradle Song		Schumann	92
Cradle Song		Hauser	95
Cradle Song		Grieg	175
Cradle Time	Wonson	Miessner	99
Crow, The	Hartford	Hartford	59
Cupboard, The	de la Mare	Miessner	9
Dame, Get Up	Mother Goose	Traditional	8
Dancing Doll		Poldini	72
Delicatessen Store	Chaffee	Protheroe	111
Dickory, Dickory, Dock	Mother Goose	Elliott	78
Did You Ever See a Lassie?		Singing Game	158
Dish-Washing Song	Turner	German	5
Doggie's Bath	Browne	Ambrose	106
Dolly's Lullaby	Hartford	Hartford	24
Dove, The	Miessner	Miessner	145
Dragon, The	Thompson	Grant-Schaefer	53
Dressed-Up Town, The	Watkins	Ambrose	126
Drum, The	Turner	German	27
Duck and the Hen, The	Clark	Russian	36
Early Spring	Fassitt	Grant-Schaefer	129
Easter Eggs	Baker	Birge	152
Easter-Time	Shepard	Wright	75
Elephant, The	Wonson	Grant-Schaefer	28
Engines	Bray	French	115
Entr'acte Music	"Rosamunde"	Schubert	54
Evening Prayer	"Hänsel and Gretel"	Humperdinck	92
Extremes	Riley	Bartholomew	162
Fair Land of Poland, The	"Bohemian Girl"	Balfe	81
Fairies' March	"Midsummer Night's Dream"	Mendelssohn	53
Farmer, The	Bray	Nursery Song	110
Feeding the Birds	Bates	Mueller	134
Fiddle and I	Miller	Miller	163
Fiddles and Horns	Bray	French	155
Field Daisy, The	Anonymous	Birge	161
Finale from Sonata in D		Haydn	87
Fire, The	Bray	Nursery Game	40
Fireman, The	Miller	Miller	107
Five and Ten Cent Store, The	Chaffee	Nursery Tune	112
Five Little White Mice	Dunning	German	144
Flag Day	Whitmore	Bugle Call	153
Flagman, The	Bray	Bray	40
Flatterer, The		Chaminade	84
Fluttering Leaves	Hartford	Hartford	58
Fly, Kite	Thompson	Bray	65
Follow the Leader	Bray	Scandinavian	16
For Our Soldiers	Decker	Lindsay	76
Foreboding of Grief		Schumann	57
Forge, The	"Siegfried"	Wagner	43
Fountain, The	Fyleman	McConathy	43
Four Seasons, The	Shepard	O'Hara	58

TITLE	AUTHOR OR SOURCE	COMPOSER OR SOURCE	PAGE
FRIENDLY COW, THE	Stevenson	Birge	141
FRIENDS FOR TEA	Bray	Bray	101
FROGS AT SCHOOL	Cooper	Birge	142
FUNNY LITTLE BUNNY	Applegarth	Loth	106
GAME, A	Nursery Rhyme	German	19
GARDENER, THE	Thompson	Ware	132
GAVOTTE		Handel	89
GAVOTTE		French	94
GAVOTTE		Goosec	172
GAVOTTE	"Don Juan"	von Gluck	175
GAVOTTE IN D		von Wilm	90
GEORGE WASHINGTON'S BIRTHDAY	Bray	Bugle Call	74
GIANTS, THE	"Rheingold"	Wagner	54
GIPSY RONDO		Haydn	82
GOING TO SCHOOL IN THE RAIN	Watkins	Loth	14
GOOD-BY SONG, A	Hartford	Hartford	15
GOOD MORNING!	Watkins	Terhune	13
GOOD MORNING, HAPPY CHILDREN		English	12
GOOD NIGHT	Houghton	Ambrose	103
GRAY PONY	Hartford	Hartford	104
GRAY SQUIRREL	Baker	Grant-Schaefer	139
GRAY SQUIRRELS	Ostrander	Ostrander	140
GREETING TO VISITORS	Shepard	O'Hara	15
HABANERA	"Carmen"	Bizet	94
HALLOWE'EN			148
HALLOWE'EN NIGHT	Thompson	Terhune	70
HAPPY AND LIGHT OF HEART	"Bohemian Girl"	Balfe	85
HAPPY CHILD, A	Greenaway	Birge	104
HAPPY JOURNEY		Behr	28
HAPPY NEW YEAR	Shepard	Grant-Schaefer	74
HARK, HARK, THE DOGS DO BARK	Mother Goose	Parker	147
HEY, DIDDLE DIDDLE	Mother Goose	Elliott	80
HOUSEKEEPING	Nursery Rhyme	Nursery Song	100
HUMPTY DUMPTY	Mother Goose	Elliott	146
HURDY-GURDY, THE	Miller	Birge	108
I AM THE WIND	Raymond	Ambrose	45
I WISH	Thompson	Grant-Schaefer	51
I'D LIKE TO BE A FARMER	Sloat	Loth	123
IF I'D AS MUCH MONEY	Mother Goose	White	114
IN FAIRYLAND	Bingham	Rogers	143
IN THE PARK	Shepard	O'Hara	43
IN THE WOOD	Shepard	O'Hara	50
INVITATION TO THE DANCE		Weber	67
IRONING DAY	Hill	Birge	7
JACK BE NIMBLE	Mother Goose	White	80
JACK-IN-THE-BOX	Bray	Russian	17
JACK-IN-THE-PULPIT	Smith	Rogers	129
JANUARY	Coleridge	German	61
JANUARY AND FEBRUARY	Rossetti	Modern Music Series	127
KING OF FRANCE, THE	Mother Goose	Elliott	147
KITTY WHITE	Mother Goose	Ambrose	138
KNIGHT OF THE HOBBY-HORSE, THE	"Scenes from Childhood"	Schumann	22
KNOCK AT THE DOOR	Nursery Rhyme	Traditional	23
KRIS KRINGLE'S TRAVELS	Best	Grant-Schaefer	72
LADY DAFFADOWN	Rossetti	Modern Music Series	130
LAKE, THE		Bennett	49
LAND OF COUNTERPANE, THE	Stevenson	Miessner	99
LARGHETTO		Schumann	57
LARGO	"Xerxes"	Handel	96
LAZY CAT, THE	Mother Goose	Elliott	33
LEAVES ARE GONE, THE	Hartford	Hartford	123
LEAVES IN AUTUMN	Grant	Terhune	122
LILY BELLS	Baker	Parker	135
LINCOLN	Dutcher	Miessner	151
LITTLE BETTY BLUE	Traditional	Miessner	164
LITTLE BUNNY RABBIT	Ostrander	Ostrander	140
LITTLE FISHES	Miller	Miller	165
LITTLE GOBLIN, THE	Thompson	Birge	51
LITTLE JACK HORNER	Mother Goose	Elliott	78
LITTLE MINUET IN G		Bach	88
LITTLE MISS MUFFET	Mother Goose	McCullough	80
LITTLE RAINDROPS	Hawkshaw	Birge	48
LITTLE RED HEN, THE	Traditional	Miessner	37
LITTLE WALTZ		Ambrose	18
LONDON BRIDGE		Singing Game	160
LOOBY LOO		Singing Game	158
LOOKING-GLASS CHILD, THE	Hartford	Hartford	103
MAKING A SNOW-MAN	Clark	Ware	63
MAKING A VALENTINE	Miessner	Miessner	152
MALBROUGH HAS GONE TO WAR		Crusaders' Song	85
MAN-IN-THE-MOON, THE	Horn	Horn	121
MARCH	Garnett	Grant-Schaefer	127
MARCH		Weber	82
MARCH	"Aida"	Verdi	20
MARCH	"Carmen"	Bizet	83
MARCH OF THE THREE KINGS (The Magi)		French	181
MARCHE HÉROÏQUE		Schubert	171
MARCHING	Bray	Bray	21
MARY, MARY, QUITE CONTRARY	Mother Goose	White	146
MAY BASKET	Miller	Miller	153
MAY DAY	Thompson	Mueller	76
MAZURKA		Chopin	184
MAZURKA RUSSE		Ganne	62
MELODY		Mendelssohn	60
MELODY IN F		Rubinstein	64
MERRY CHRISTMAS	Hartford	Hartford	149
MERRY-GO-ROUND, THE	Baker	Swedish	32
MILITARY MARCH		Schubert	173
MINUET		French	95
MINUET	"Symphony in Bb"	Haydn	177
MINUET	"Don Juan"	Mozart	88
MINUETTO		Handel	176
"MINUTE" WALTZ		Chopin	56
MIX A PANCAKE	Rossetti	Halle	100
MOCKING BIRD, THE	Morgan	Miessner	136
MONKEY THE	Morgan	Ambrose	33
MOOLEY COW RED	Baker	Loth	37
MOONLIGHT	Decker	Birge	46
MOONLIGHT SCENE		Reinecke	52
MORNING	Stockman	Miessner	2
MORNING PRAYER	Turner	Modern Music Series	14
MOTHER AND FATHER	Bray	Bray	98
MOTOR CAR, THE	Miller	Miller	116
MOUNTAIN, THE	Shepard	O'Hara	50
MOUSE COUSINS	Rossetti	Modern Music Series	169
MUFFIN MAN, THE		Singing Game	158
MULBERRY BUSH, THE		Singing Game	159
MURMURING ZEPHYRS		Jensen	45
MY BABY-BO	Richards	Miessner	97
MY DICKY BIRD	Harris	Brickner	105
MY DOG	Wonson	Findlay	138
MY FIRE ENGINE	Wonson	Protheroe	26
MY FLUTE	Miessner	Miessner	26
MY HEN	Bokeloh	Protheroe	143
MY KITE	Grant	Protheroe	120
MY PONY	Thompson	Protheroe	32
MY SCOOTER	Thompson	Grant-Schaefer	157
MY SHINGLE BOAT	Wonson	Miessner	161
MY TEDDY BEAR	Wonson	Grant-Schaefer	26
MY ZITHER	Powell	Italian	166
NAZARETH		Gounod	73
NEW BONNET, THE	Wonson	Bray	164
NEW YEAR, THE	Anonymous	Protheroe	150
NEWSBOY	Hartford	Hartford	108
NINETEEN BIRDS	Mother Goose	Elliott	156
NOCTURNE	"Midsummer Night's Dream"	Mendelssohn	57
NORTH WIND DOTH BLOW, THE	Mother Goose	Elliott	124
NORTHERN SONG		Schumann	178
NOVEMBER	Anonymous	Birge	60
NOW GOOD-NIGHT	Bray	Taps	3
NOW THE TIME HAS COME FOR PLAY	Old Rhyme	German	168
O TENDER MOON	"Faust"	Gounod	93
OAK TREES	Moore	Mueller	133
OH, HERE IS MISS PUSSY	Child Life in Song	Parker	106
OLD KING COLE	Mother Goose	English	147
OLD MOTHER WIND	Chinese Rhyme	Ware	46
OLD WOMAN, THE	Chinese Rhyme	Birge	110
ON THE BUS	Applegarth	Protheroe	115

TITLE	AUTHOR OR SOURCE	COMPOSER OR SOURCE	PAGE
On the Way to School	Thompson	Loth	109
Organ Man, The	Porter	Grant-Schaefer	39
Oriole's Nest, The	Morgan	Ware	137
Our Flag	Bray	Bugle Call	76
Owl, The	Hartford	Hartford	136
Pansies	Bates	Miessner	133
Paper Dolls	Wonson	Bray	24
Parade, The	Hartford	Hartford	21
Pet Bird, The	Thompson	McConathy	6
Pifferari, Les		Gounod	30
Pigeons	Morgan	Miessner	6
Piggy-wig and Piggy-wee	Miessner	Miessner	38
Pirates' March	"Pirates of Penzance"	Sullivan	81
Playing Ball	Thompson	Ambrose	18
Playing Circus	Decker	Birge	17
Playing in the Band	Laird	Miessner	16
Playing Indian	Thompson	Lindsay	157
Playing the Bugle		French	27
Playing with Baby	Nursery Rhyme	Wright	3
Politeness	Decker	Ambrose	14
Polly's Piano		Modern Music Series	169
Poor Snow-Man, The	Decker	Birge	62
Postman, The	Thompson	Ambrose	42
Postman's Whistle, The	Decker	Birge	42
Puss	Garnett	Grant-Schaefer	30
Rabbit, A	Roberts	Miller	139
Rain	Fassitt	Lindsay	117
Rain in April	Hammond	Ambrose	129
Rain in Summer	Dunbar	Loth	130
Rainy Day	Bray	Loth	48
Ready for School	Bray	Mueller	12
Real Work	Dunbar	Grant-Schaefer	7
Reason Why, The	German	German	170
Riding	Wonson	Miessner	16
Right Way, The	Pratt	Birge	13
Ring, The		Elliott	160
River, The	Bokeloh	Findlay	118
Robin	Anonymous	Bray	167
Robin, The	Alma-Tadema	Birge	132
Rock-a-Bye	Bray	McConathy	2
Rockaway Land	Bokeloh	Birge	97
Rocking Horse, The	Fox	Birge	24
Roses from the South (Second Strain)		Strauss	180
Round and Round the Village		Singing Game	159
Safety First	Miller	Miller	11
Salute the Flag	Bray	Army Call	148
Sandman, The	Clark	Birge	4
Sea, The	Wynne	Protheroe	118
Sea Song from the Shore	Riley	Bartholomew	119
Secret, The	Gainsborough	Parker	134
See-Saw	Nursery Rhyme	Bray	23
See-Saw, Margery Daw	Mother Goose	Elliott	79
Shear the Sheep	Traditional	Elliott	142
Ships	Morgan	Terhune	119
Shoe the Old Horse	Mother Goose	Spanish	39
Signs of Autumn	The Modern Music Series	Wright	58
Silent Night		Gruber	74
Silk Worm, The	Foresman	Modern Music Series	169
Sing Me a Song	Rossetti	Rogers	157
Sing, Said the Mother	Traditional	Appalachian	131
Skating	Miessner	Miessner	125
Sleeping Dolls	Willard	Ambrose	25
Slumber Song		Schumann	184
Snowbirds	Bray	Russian	61
Snowflake Feathers	Bray	Loth	126
Snowflakes	Dodge	Protheroe	124
Snowflakes		Wright	62
Snowman, The	Miller	Miller	125
Soldiers' Chorus	"Il Trovatore"	Verdi	176
Sonata in D		Haydn	171
Sonatina		Schumann	172
Spinner, The	Garnett	Ambrose	4
Spring	Rossetti	Ware	128

TITLE	AUTHOR OR SOURCE	COMPOSER OR SOURCE	PAGE
Spring Flowers	Fassitt	Ware	128
Spring Song	Thompson	Rogers	65
Spring Song	"Songs without Words"	Mendelssohn	64
Squirrel, The		Ambrose	31
Star, The		Modern Music Series	170
Stephanie Gavotte		Czibulka	55
Storm, The	Bray	Lindsay	46
Street Boys' Parade	"Carmen"	Bizet	22
Street-Cleaner Man, The	Applegarth	Miessner	109
Summer and Winter	Foresman	Nursery Songs	122
Summer Days	Hartford	Hartford	67
Summer Night	Newbolt	Grant-Schaefer	68
Sun, The	Thompson	Ambrose	47
Sunset	Baker	Schuler	168
Swing Song	Wonson	Miessner	156
Swinging	Thompson	Mueller	132
Taddy Pole and Polly Wog	Nursery Rhyme	Bray	36
Tap, Tap, Tap!	Clark	Loth	68
Telephone, The	Hartford	Hartford	107
Ten Pretty Maidens	Traditional	Miessner	165
Thanksgiving	Shepard	O'Hara	71
Thanksgiving Day	Dutcher	Miessner	149
Theme from Sonata		Mozart	183
Theme from the Sonata in A		Mozart	50
Theme from "First Mazurka"		Saint-Saëns	29
Things I Like	Miessner	Miessner	13
Thirsty Butterfly	Watkins	Terhune	69
Three Little Kittens	Traditional	English	37
Time to Get Up	Turner	Bugle Call	10
Tin Soldiers and Pussy	Hartford	Hartford	30
To Market	Mother Goose	French	17
Toreador Song	"Carmen"	Bizet	90
Town Clock, The		French	114
Traffic Cop, The	Bray	Protheroe	44
Traffic Light, The	Bray	Ambrose	44
Trolley Car, The	Clark	Grant-Schaefer	41
Trolley-Man, The	Morgan	Lindsay	110
Trot, Trot	Butts	Miessner	3
Turkish March		Beethoven	91
Turkish March	"Sonata in A Major"	Mozart	174
Two Little Blackbirds	Mother Goose	German	23
Valentines	Whitmore	Schubert	151
Valse		Chopin	59
Valse		Chopin	179
Variations on a French Melody		Mozart	84
Waggley Dog, The	Dunbar	Protheroe	139
Waltz from "Love's Dream after the Ball"		Czibulka	19
Waltz, No. 2		Brahms	96
Washing Day	Wonson	Birge	7
Washington and the Flag	Bray	Miessner	151
Wee Ducky Doddles	Applegarth	Ambrose	29
When Cats Get Up	Nursery Rhyme	French	105
When Daddy Comes Home	Applegarth	Miessner	101
When the Stars	"St. Nicholas"	Garrett	121
Which Way Does the Wind Blow?	Aikin	German	61
Whirl, Top, Whirl!	Thompson	Grant-Schaefer	25
Who Likes the Rain?	Bates	Grant-Schaefer	141
Who'll Be My Valentine?	Decker	Bray	75
Who's at the Door?	Bray	Birge	8
Wild Rider, The		Schumann	86
Willow Cats, The	Widdemer	French	127
Wind, The	Traditional	English	120
Wind Mill, The	Nursery Rhyme	Miessner	166
Wise Little Gold Fish	Applegarth	Miessner	6
Wishing Star, The	Wonson	Miessner	47
Work and Play	Rossetti	Ware	102
Yankee Doodle		Old Song	154
Young Engineer, The	Morgan	French	40
Zoo, The	Moore Miller	Grant-Schaefer	144